A TEACHER'S GUIDE TO

COGNITIVE TYPE THEORY & LEARNING STYLE

Carolyn Mamchur

Association for Supervision and Curriculum Development
Alexandria, Virginia

ASCD

Association for Supervision and Curriculum Development
1250 N. Pitt Street • Alexandria, Virginia 22314-1453
Telephone: 1-800-933-2723 or 703-549-9110 • Fax: 703-299-8631

Gene R. Carter, *Executive Director*
Michelle Terry, *Assistant Executive Director, Program Development*
Ronald S. Brandt, *Assistant Executive Director*
Nancy Modrak, *Director, Publications*
Julie Houtz, *Managing Editor of Books*
Kathie Felix, *Associate Editor*
Gary Bloom, *Director, Editorial, Design, and Production Services*
Karen Monaco, *Senior Designer*
Tracey A. Smith, *Production Coordinator*
Dina Murray, *Production Assistant*
Cindy Stock, *Desktop Publisher*

Printed in the United States of America.

December 1996 member book (p). ASCD Premium, Comprehensive, and Regular members periodically receive ASCD books as part of their membership benefits. No. FY97-3.
ASCD Stock No.: 196275
ASCD member price: $15.95   Nonmember price: $18.95

Library of Congress Cataloging-in-Publication Data

Mamchur, Carolyn Marie, 1943–
    A teacher's guide to cognitive type theory and learning style / Carolyn Mamchur. p. cm.
    Includes bibliographical references and index.
    ISBN 0-87120-278-6
    1. Learning, Psychology of. 2. Cognitive styles in children. 3. Cognitive styles in children—Testing. 4. Typology (Psychology) 5. Teaching. I. Title.
    LB1060.M3242 1996
    370.15'2—dc21   96-45842
                                                                    CIP

00 99 98 97 96   5 4 3 2 1

Dedicated to
Dorothy Farnell, teacher, friend.

Acknowledgments

Thanks to all the students and teachers who helped me to understand the real power of learning style theory as we worked together developing the ideas and materials that informed this book. Thanks to Cindy Reid who, with her students at Holy Cross, worked on developing and testing OPTIONS with her usual insight and electrifying enthusiasm. Thanks to the team of experts whose ideas, talents, anxious pride, and generous energy made this book a pleasure to write: Ron Brandt, ASCD assistant executive director; Mark Goldberg, acquisitions editor; Eileen Mallory and Candida Mazza, desktop publishers; and Elizabeth Carefoot, graphic artist. Dear friends. All. Thanks to Mickey, my guardian angel.

CAROLYN MARIE MAMCHUR
Vancouver, British Columbia

A Teacher's Guide to Cognitive Type Theory and Learning Style

Introduction: Learning Style and the Classroom Teacher

The mandate for classroom teachers of the 1990s has become increasingly difficult: be parent, police officer, caregiver, instructor of principles and skills and attitudes. And do it all with expertise, with wisdom, and with attention to individual needs and differences.

Oh, okay!

Today's classroom teachers need all the special help they can get. This book is intended to help teachers understand natural learning style patterns and behaviors and handle them in a way that empowers students and teachers both.

Understanding individual learning preferences and differences is an increasingly popular and useful tool, serving teachers in four ways. First, teachers have a method to teach that is diverse and adaptive enough to meet the various learning style needs of students who are not necessarily oriented toward schooling. Second, teachers can indicate to students that they care about the individuality and integrity of each learner. Third, because learning style is related to teaching style, teachers can better understand their own teaching styles and strengths and weaknesses. And fourth, teachers can gain insight into how they work together in this particular world we call school.

Selecting the Instrument

The first task in determining learning style patterns is to choose a good instrument that measures or indicates particular patterns. There are several on the market, all urging the prospective client to choose one over the others. It is the responsibility of the educator to select the appropriate instrument. The following criteria have served me well in training teachers and researchers to examine learning style theories and instruments.

1

1. Personal Response. Are the learning style attributes and personality characteristics described in the instrument meaningful to the reader? Do they make sense? Do they ring true?

2. Theoretical Background. Did the instrument grow out of a sound theoretical base? Has the instrument been carefully researched? Are the research and the theory reported in language that is easily understood?

3. Expense. Can you afford not only the instrument and its interpretation, but the consultation necessary to put the information to good use? Is there enough implementation literature available to learn on your own?

4. Complexity of Information. Is the information too simple, or too complex? If it is too complex, it may require too much time or expert consultation to use. Are the need and time restraints, as well as the degree of sophistication of the user, suitable for the degree of complexity?

5. Ability to Implement. Once the information is made available, can changes based on the findings be implemented in a meaningful way in the classroom? Is the information practical and relevant? Will it make a difference?

6. Multiple Uses. Can the information gained from the instrument and the consultation be used for more than one purpose, such as personal development, team teaching, teacher training, and improvement of staff relationships?

Jungian Psychological Type

In 25 years of study and research in the area of teacher training and learning style theories, I have found few instruments that

meet all six criteria. Because of its complexity, its integrity, and its multilevel usefulness, my favorite instrument is the Myers-Briggs Type Indicator, developed by Isabel Myers (1962) and based on the theories of Carl Jung.

Jung made a major contribution to the ability to understand self by dividing all human behavior into two basic categories: perception and judgment. His theory is that we are constantly choosing between the open act of perceiving (or finding out, discovering) and the closed act of judging (or taking action, deciding, evaluating).

This simplification of activity is the basis of Jungian type theory. A perceiver likes to spend more time in perceiving activities, a judger in judging activities. Jung maintained that individuals prefer to perceive either through their senses or their intuition, and prefer to make judgments either through their thinking or feeling processes.

Although all four functions—sensing, intuition, thinking, and feeling—are present in every individual, one is dominant or most favored, one is auxiliary and ranks as the second most used function, and the third is the tertiary function, which is less often exercised and demands more energy to use. The fourth is a person's inferior function. The inferior function, sometimes called the shadow function, is the most tyrannical and immature function and is the person's weak spot. Only with maturity, reflection, and conscious use can the inferior function serve the individual, providing inspiration and renewed energy. This process is usually reserved for the latter part of our lives and is called individuation. It is sometimes useful to think of the functions as a large Z pattern, as shown in Figure 1.

■ **E**xtraversion

■ **I**ntroversion

■ **S**ensing

■ i**N**tuition

■ **T**hinking

■ **F**eeling

■ **J**udging

■ **P**erceiving

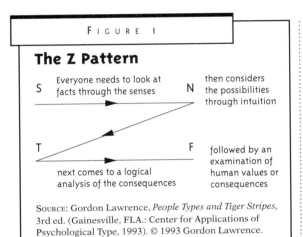

FIGURE 1

The Z Pattern

S — Everyone needs to look at facts through the senses → N — then considers the possibilities through intuition

T — next comes to a logical analysis of the consequences → F — followed by an examination of human values or consequences

SOURCE: Gordon Lawrence, *People Types and Tiger Stripes*, 3rd ed. (Gainesville, FLA.: Center for Applications of Psychological Type, 1993). © 1993 Gordon Lawrence.

Jung added the final dimension of extraversion and introversion to his psychological descriptions. He hypothesized from observation and study that those who prefer to get energy in an extraverted way will extravert their dominant function and introvert all the other functions; those preferring to get energy in an introverted way will introvert their dominant function and extravert all the rest.

Until Isabel Myers developed the Myers-Briggs Type Indicator, it was difficult to determine which preferences we had and which we extraverted or introverted; years of psychoanalysis provided the only reliable answers. Psychological type theory, as further defined by Myers, might be viewed as shown in Figure 2 on page 4.

Psychological Type Preferences and Learning Style

Awareness and selection of an instrument is the first phase in using knowledge of learning style in the workplace. I always recommend that teachers use the instrument as learners, examining their own learning style until they become familiar with the concepts.

Next will come the more sophisticated level of evaluating how difficult it will be to adapt one's own methods to the different modes of learning. It is very natural to teach in the same way we learn. It may be difficult for us to believe that others could learn in a way that is foreign and difficult for us. Because of an honest desire to do the best job, some teachers will avoid the very strategies that others need.

It is essential that teachers be patient and tolerant with themselves. Changes come slowly. Although this book is designed to help teachers develop skills for meeting the needs of all students, we must remember that every teacher has a natural, comfortable style that also must be respected. Teachers cannot lose their identity in attending to others.

Informed Choice

From a position of remembered innocence and progressively growing awareness, I invite you to use type theory and this book. Every day, I learn from the gifts that type theory offers.

When I marched off so proudly, so confidently to Gainesville, Florida, in 1976 to earn a doctorate in education, I'd never heard of Jungian type theory, never consciously considered learning styles, and never spoken the words "individual differences." Of course I hadn't yet discovered Isabel Myers or Gordon Lawrence or Mary McCaulley. I hadn't worked with them, embraced their teaching, studied their ideas, or performed my own research. Had you asked me back then, I would have insisted that I recognized my students as being different from one another and tried to meet

> FIGURE 2

The Eight Psychological Type Preferences

Does the person's interest flow mainly to the

E — outer world of actions, objects, and persons?

EXTRAVERSION

inner world of concepts and ideas? — **I**

INTROVERSION

Does the person prefer to perceive

S — the immediate, real, solid facts of experience?

SENSING

the possibilities, meanings, and relationships of experience? — **N**

INTUITION

Does the person prefer to make judgments or decisions

T — objectively and impersonally, analyzing facts and ordering them, in terms of cause and effect?

THINKING

subjectively and personally, weighing values for the importance of choices for oneself and other people? — **F**

FEELING

Does the person prefer to live

J — in a planned, orderly way, aiming to regulate and control events?

JUDGMENT

in a flexible, spontaneous way, aiming to understand and to adapt to events? — **P**

PERCEPTION

SOURCE: Mary H. McCaulley, *Four Preferences Are Scored to Arrive at a Person's Type* (Gainesville: Typology Laboratory, University of Florida, 1974). © 1976, 1988 Center for Applications of Psychological Type.

their individual needs. Yes, then I would have said I *did* meet their individual needs.

Had you asked me how I accomplished this, I could have answered only after much worried thought, because my actions, the things I did in the classroom, came way before my ability to talk about them or put labels on them. And the answer I might have come up with was that I gave my students choices.

It has always made sense to me that people work best when they are given

■ **E**xtraversion
■ **I**ntroversion
■ **S**ensing
■ **iN**tuition
■ **T**hinking
■ **F**eeling
■ **J**udging
■ **P**erceiving

choices. School, being serious hard work, demands that those folks working in a classroom be given as many choices as possible. Somehow, I came to the teaching profession with that belief, and it hasn't really changed much.

Giving students choices remains a basic credo that dominates what I do as a teacher. The difference now is that I want to give my students *informed* choices. As a young teacher with a generous nature, but only one year of teachers college, I lacked *expertise*. It was a major omission. I've spent the last 30 years trying to acquire the kinds of knowledge that will help me to offer my students—and myself—informed choices.

Studying in Florida was a key point in my search for sound theory that could lead to practical knowledge, which I could then apply to the classroom. It was in Florida that I was introduced to type theory. It was in Florida that I learned a systematic method for really understanding how my students and my colleagues preferred to receive information and make judgments.

I left Florida to design curriculum and work as a teacher-therapist with what were then called juvenile delinquent girls. Today they might be called emotionally or socially challenged female youths. Whatever the label, those young women presented problems I hadn't planned to face. I applied everything I knew. I used type theory, not only in designing curriculum but in meeting the basic needs of the damaged 14-year-olds in my charge. I combined type theory and needs theory and discovered that type theory was helpful for more than deciding how to teach students to read and write and do math. Type theory helped me see how different students feel safe and loved, and how they satisfy their needs for power and for pleasure.

I returned to Florida and earned an Ed.D. with Gordon Lawrence, while developing an observation instrument to determine extraversion and introversion. (I had been stung by the type theory bug.) I came back to Canada, taught at the university level, and conducted research on type theory; I wrote a book about it, gave a thousand workshops, and journeyed to the Jung Institute near Zurich to further explore Jung's work.

The single most useful piece of knowledge I have acquired in my search to give informed choices to students is Jungian type theory. It is my purpose in this book to give you everything you need to begin the job of using type theory immediately in your classroom.

The shape of the book is straightforward. In Part One, I systematically describe each of the eight choices defined by the Myers-Briggs Type Indicator, the instrument developed by Myers and Briggs to determine type in adult individuals:

1. **Introversion or Extraversion.** How do you prefer to focus your energy and interest? Outwardly, in an *extraverted* fashion, or inwardly, in an *introverted* fashion?

2. **Sensing or Intuitive.** How do you like to give and receive information? In a straightforward, realistic *sensing* way, or in a more complex, connective, *intuitive* way?

3. **Thinking or Feeling.** How do you like to make decisions? In an objective, analytical, *thinking* manner, or in a more subjective, values-oriented, *feeling* manner?

4. **Judging or Perceiving.** How do you like to function in the world? In an organized, purpose-driven, *judging* style, or a more flexible, experience-driven, *perceiving* style?

The manner in which I present these choices is designed to meet the needs of all types. For the sensing, thinking types who want the straight goods, I simply define each choice by answering these questions:

1. What are these things, extraversion, introversion, sensing, and so forth?

2. How do extraversion, introversion, and so forth, affect behavior?

3. How does each type factor influence the way one interacts, communicates, teaches?

4. How does each type factor influence learning preferences?

5. How can you, the teacher, design curriculum to satisfy the various learning preferences?

I also answer other important questions: What is this particular aspect of type? How does it affect behavior? How does it affect the teacher's choices? How does it influence learning preferences? How do you develop curriculum using knowledge of those preferences? And I provide checklists of informed choices for you to make. You may come to recognize this as an Introverted Sensing Thinking Judging (ISTJ) style of presenting information.

Each of the first eight chapters concludes with a "Close-up" section written in a narrative style. The Close-ups are case studies that look at real people in real classrooms using type theory in various circumstances for various purposes. They present curriculum and relationship issues affecting the teacher or the student. The Close-ups are designed to answer some of the questions that have come up in my teaching of type in hundreds of workshops across the country. You may come to recognize this approach as an Extraverted

Intuiting Feeling Perceiving (ENFP) style of presenting information.

I've tried to answer questions by giving real-life examples that allow for personal extrapolation of the information. Although I have composited several time frames or experiences into one and changed the names of individuals and schools, I always strive to present the truth as I have experienced it over the years.

Part Two, "Special Readings," contains related readings on learning style and type theory. The first chapter in this section is "A Playground for Teachers"; it is a chapter free of the responsibility of applying knowledge of type theory to the classroom. This chapter invites you to familiarize yourself with type by determining your own preferences and by playing with type theory where the stakes are not very high. If you want to read this chapter before reading the rest of this book, go ahead. I usually begin my workshops on type theory by having teachers determine their own preferences and then work through various tasks and exercises to playfully familiarize themselves with the ideas. The exercises also give teachers the opportunity to test the validity of these ideas for themselves in the arena of everyday life.

Chapter 11, "Temperaments and Teaching," focuses on the motivational patterns of different types. This section of the book looks at some of the reasons tempers or tears may visit the staff room.

Chapter 12, "Don't Let the Moon Break Your Heart," first appeared as an article in *Educational Leadership* in 1984. Because so many teachers have expressed such appreciation for this piece, which looks at the reluctant learner, I have included it here. It provides an intimate look at the type of

Introduction: Learning Style and the Classroom Teacher

7

■ **E**xtraversion
■ **I**ntroversion
■ **S**ensing
■ i**N**tuition
■ **T**hinking
■ **F**eeling
■ **J**udging
■ **P**erceiving

learner most likely to drop out of school. I offer this chapter with special affection because it focuses on a reluctant learner very dear to my heart, my daughter Michelle.

I would feel remiss if I did not include, in a book on learning style, a word about the potential dangers and benefits housed by any system that labels others. Chapter 13, "Poor Uncle Harry," examines the positive and negative potential of putting labels on behaviors.

Learning style, though by its nature benign, is still a classification or labeling system. "Poor Uncle Harry" presents my own experience of how a label can cause pain and can also release you from that pain. Like anything else, type theory is only as wise and as useful as the person using it allows it to be. The final responsibility lies in the user, not the tool.

Finally, I have included OPTIONS, an instrument designed to help teachers and students determine student type preferences. The type code students choose when they answer the questions posed in the instrument may or may not be their final life choice; type is developmental and young people, especially in elementary school, are still trying on the various types to see how they fit.

Although Jung says we select our preferences very early, we do not always display a real preference until our late teens. It is essential to remember that type theory is not a trait theory; nor does it suggest that individuals inherit specific traits. It is a theory that looks at *process*, at how one prefers to *do* things. The process of discovery and self-awareness is a life-long adventure, and OPTIONS is a way to explore present preferences that influence the learning style your students may prefer right now.

Most young students show an early preference for sensation and feeling as indicated by both OPTIONS and the Murphy Meisgeier Type Indicator for Children (Meisgeier and Murphy 1987). This finding isn't different from the findings of other theorists examining child development. Sensation is, in Piagetian terms, very similar to the concrete operational mode so natural to young people. Intuition, a more complex way to see relationships between things, usually follows the concrete stage. However, I must admit my bias: I believe that much of the research and theory regarding the developmental stages of child development is primitive and has not yet really considered individual differences. Therefore, even though such terms as "concrete operational" may be useful, they are not definitive.

Our understanding of type and children will grow immensely as teachers become more aware of type theory and begin using it in classrooms while observing students and coming up with their own theories and conclusions. To date, most of the research on Jung's ideas has focused on adults and adult behavior. Although many type researchers believe certain type preferences, such as intuition, can be consistently observed as a preference in young children, the observation of children's type preferences remains an area worthy of new investigation. I believe teachers, more than any other group, can contribute to this research.

They may begin to answer such questions as "Why do young students report a preference for feeling over thinking?" It may be that thinking takes longer to develop

---

FIGURE 3

Average North American High School Population

Extravert	75%	Introvert	25%
Sensing	80%	Intuitive	20%
Thinking (m)	60%	Feeling (f)	60%
(f)	40%	(m)	40%
Judging	55%	Perceiving	45%

NOTE: MALE (M), FEMALE (F)
SOURCE: MYERS 1985

---

than feeling, for example, or it may be that we use feeling language with children. When is the last time you heard a child being asked to stand back and logically analyze the data? The language of decision making we most often use is the language of "right and wrong," "good and bad," "please mommy," and "do what your father says."

Once students reach high school, definite patterns of preferences seem to emerge. Figure 3 shows the pattern in the average North American high school.

Because any new system contains its own terms and definitions, and because these can be so irritatingly confusing when you are learning a new system, I have included a concise glossary of definitions at the back of the book on page 130.

I hope that this introduction to type theory unravels its mysteries, reveals the range of choices, and marks a promising beginning. It may provide a helpful clarifier for those of you who have already begun the journey of using Jung's types to create a richer, fuller world.

I hope, too, that this approach is as satisfying for you as it has been for me and that as you continue to learn you'll share your knowledge with your colleagues and students. Type theory is like a great recipe; it begs to be shared. Sit around the table, pour the coffee, pass the cake, and begin.

Part 1

The Basics
of Type Theory

1

The Extraverted Learner

▶ **What is extraversion?**

An outward focusing of energy.

▶ **How does extraversion affect behavior?**

It causes the person to seek outside influences as a source of energy, pleasure, and satisfaction.

▶ **How does extraversion affect the way one interacts, communicates, and teaches?**

It causes the person to enjoy open, active interactions, to become absorbed in activities, and to have a high tolerance for crowds, noise, and public appearances. Restless and cooperative, the extraverted teacher wants to have a busy classroom. She can tolerate a variety of simultaneous activities and exudes energy, excitement, and enthusiasm. She often shares with her students aspects of her life outside of school because she is so enthusiastic about her activities.

▶ How does a preference for extraversion translate into learning preferences?

1. Extraverted students like to think out loud. They really don't know what they know until they have the chance to talk it out. Talking is a clarifying process.

2. Extraverted students learn by doing. They are action-oriented and prefer hands-on experience.

3. Extraverted students like to learn together. They enjoy sharing ideas and tasks.

4. Extraverted students enjoy variety. They prefer to experience a whole range of activities, focusing finally on a select few.

5. Extraverted students need feedback from the teacher and from peers. They need to know how they are doing.

▶ How does the teacher respond to these preferences?

The teacher creates a classroom in which extraverts have some opportunity to talk and discuss, to present their ideas, and to move. She involves students in group work, practical activities, making things, putting on plays, or discussion corners. She creates a space where students can be actively, sometimes noisily, engaged in projects.

The teacher makes sure extraverts know what's expected of them and tells them how well they are doing. She incorporates positive feedback, either her own or through students' peers, into the design of all programs. She encourages students to ask questions and give opinions. She teaches them to be polite, caring, and constructive. She never allows cruelty.

Close-up: Extraversion

When Anna Friesen discovered type theory, she was excited. As an extravert, she wanted to put her new knowledge into practice right away. The first thing she did was to use **OPTIONS** to find out the types of all her students. A firm believer in the idea that you should let students in on your knowledge and sources, she started to teach them about type theory the day she had them determine their preferences.

Jungian theory professes that we choose extraversion or introversion very early—in fact, in infanthood. Experts who observe young children agree on what they think they are observing: consistent extraverted or introverted behavior.

Ms. Friesen was careful to explain to students that type selection is a develop-

The Extraverted Learner ■ **E**xtraversion
■ **I**ntroversion

13 ■ **S**ensing

■ i**N**tuition

■ **T**hinking

■ **F**eeling

■ **J**udging

■ **P**erceiving

mental process and that as 6th graders they were still growing into the adult persons they would become. She was delighted by how quickly her students grasped the ideas and understood how type influenced the way they preferred to work. But she was careful to explain that in this system extraversion and introversion mean more than being talkative or shy; the terms also relate to how one likes to focus energy, how one likes to work, and what interests a person.

As the students explored type ideas and became more aware of their choices in the way they did things, Ms. Friesen took a brave step. She divided her students into extraverted and introverted groups and had them come up with ideal working conditions for their group. She also had them list things that were going on in her classroom that were unsatisfactory or difficult for them to do.

Ms. Friesen was surprised by the results.

Introverts suddenly had a lot to say. Encouraged by the structure of the teacher's invitation and bolstered by the comments of others who felt as they did, these students talked about how they felt about what happened in the classroom.

First on the students' list of complaints was "surprise speeches," Ms. Friesen's practice of having students draw topics from a hat and just "talk away" impromptu style for a minute or two. Unhappy with the local practice of having students spend months preparing for and delivering long speeches in a regional contest each spring, Ms. Friesen met the department of education's demand for speech training in her own extraverted way. It was something she thought her students loved. She was good at making up interesting topics. So were they. Weren't they?

The introverts feared this practice. They needed time to think things through on their own, and Ms. Friesen wasn't giving them any. Introverts need time to rehearse everything, even answers to simple questions. They certainly needed to rehearse a minute-long talk. However, they didn't enjoy the formal, competitive, copy-from-the-encyclopedia speeches either.

What to do? Speech giving was part of the curriculum, and it was mandated that students learn this skill. Ms. Friesen and her students decided that the speeches would be less formal and become more of a teaching task. Students would show one another how to do something they liked to do, such as fly fishing, needlepoint, or baking a cake.

Introverts feel more confident when they express a sense of genuine interest in and knowledge about their topic. They like to use aids (slides, overheads, demonstration utensils) while they are giving their presentations. And they need time to prepare: rehearsal time.

The new "show and teach" speeches seemed to solve the problem. Introverts learned to do an extraverted task in a way most conducive to their own needs. What's more, they were helping to design their curriculum, to take charge of choosing their topics and their methods of presentation. Both extraverts and introverts enjoy that sense of involvement, of having some power over their own learning environments.

Ms. Friesen's extraverted students were generally happy with things as they were. Because their teacher was extraverted, they had plenty of opportunity to practice their extraversion. They found silent reading, another districtwide requirement, to be the most taxing thing they had to do. They wondered if they could examine alternative methods of study.

Ms. Friesen was excited by what the extraverts said about silent reading. She and her students lived in Tampa, Florida, but had access to type theory information from the PK Yonge Laboratory School, which is associated with the University of Florida in Gainesville, where Helen Guttinger had done a lot of research in reading. Ms. Friesen and her students decided to replicate some of that research.

"Let your students become theorists, researchers" was another of Ms. Friesen's beliefs. She had discovered that idea by reading *Beginning with Ourselves* (Hunt 1987). It was a book that influenced many of her teaching decisions. In true extraverted style, Ms. Friesen liked to apply several theories at once, creating her own unique combination of ideas.*

Ms. Friesen and her students devised "talking booths" at the back of the classroom where extraverts (and introverts who felt like it) could meet midway during their silent reading period to discuss what they were reading. They kept records of reading scores and attitudes toward silent reading. They discovered that extraverts improved their reading skills and their concentration when they had the chance to discuss midstream; they also discovered that extraverts preferred to discuss after their reading had been completed. The whole project was very successful. Ms. Friesen and her students felt engaged and in control of what they were doing.

Ms. Friesen's belief was that students can perform sophisticated decision making and make good, informed choices when they are given the knowledge or resources to do so. She tried to live by those convictions and found type theory useful in helping her do that.

---

*A wonderful source of information is the Center for Applications of Psychological Type (CAPT), 2815 N.W. 13th St., Suite 401, Gainesville, FL 32609.

2

The Introverted Learner

▶ **What is introversion?**

An inward focusing of energy.

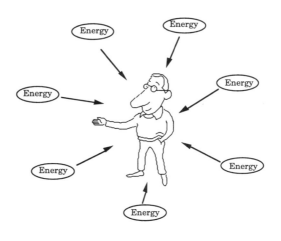

▶ **How does introversion affect behavior?**

It causes the person to look inward for sources of energy, satisfaction, and safety.

▶ **How does introversion affect the way one interacts, communicates, and teaches?**

It causes the person to enjoy intense, focused relationships and events. Cautious, considerate, and thoughtful, the introvert prefers a well-ordered classroom in which students work quietly on one project at a time. Intolerant of noise and interruption, the introverted teacher seeks to protect the individual's need for privacy by creating a dignified, respectful classroom atmosphere.

▶ How does a preference for introversion translate into learning style?

1. Introverted students need to think everything through, inside their heads, before they risk responding in front of others. Introverts are often the quiet, thoughtful members of a classroom. They prefer to volunteer answers to questions, rather than be asked a question directly. When they trust their teacher and are confident of their knowledge, they can surprise everyone with unexpected and intense responses.

2. Introverted students are private beings. Their deep and easily violated sense of privacy extends to the learning space. Introverts need a sense of place and a feeling of ownership over that space. They prefer that no one else inhabit that space. If learning supplies are to be left in the learning space, they must be left undisturbed. They appreciate quiet, uninterrupted work where concentrated energy focuses on one thing at a time.

3. Introverted students are self-motivated. They deeply resent anyone "looking over their shoulder" as they learn. They want clear instructions to follow and the opportunity to explore ideas without supervision. If they need help, they prefer to watch an expert, read a resource, or watch a video. Having to learn and perform simultaneously is trying for introverts, who want to learn enough to be able to do the task fairly well before they have to try it, especially in front of their peers or even an instructor.

▶ How does the teacher respond to these preferences?

The teacher designs a classroom that allows introverts time and space to think and learn. This can be accomplished by redesigning the classroom with carrels for private study, individually assigned work spaces, and small-group study areas set off from the larger teaching space. The teacher can also use questioning methods that allow introverts time to reflect and rehearse before answering, so they don't feel put on the spot.

The Introverted Learner   ■ **E**xtraversion

17   ■ **I**ntroversion

■ **S**ensing

■ i**N**tuition

■ **T**hinking

■ **F**eeling

■ **J**udging

■ **P**erceiving

The teacher would be wise to make available several resources for introverts to use independently. Videotapes, manuals, and books enable the introvert to independently review any concepts demonstrated in class. Introverts often enjoy working with a peer whom they trust.

Close-up: Introversion

Harvey Gilden, an introvert, wasn't nearly as excited about type theory as his colleague, Anna Friesen. Harvey taught 7th grade in the same school as Anna. He didn't want to rush into anything, and he certainly didn't want to lose control of the classroom the way he feared Anna might be doing. Harvey wanted to be sure of what he was doing. As an introverted sensing type, he liked to learn by carefully observing over an extended period of time.

He chose to learn about type theory and about his students' learning styles by using AORO (short for "Action-Oriented, Reflection-Oriented"), an observation instrument designed to help teachers determine extraversion and introversion in students (Mamchur 1984, pp. 223–229; see Figures 2.1 and 2.2). Action-Oriented in essence defines the behaviors you will see an extraverted student displaying. Reflection-Oriented defines introverted behavior.

Harvey was content to start with this one dimension. He preferred to do one thing at a time and he'd read that extraversion and introversion were the easiest aspects of type theory to recognize and deal with. Harvey was by nature cautious and conservative. He read the instructions carefully:

Specific Instructions for Using AORO (Action-Oriented, Reflection-Oriented)

Learn a New Way of Seeing Students

The actual process of using the instrument will help you learn more about your students and how they are functioning. AORO is designed to help you, the teacher, develop a new frame of reference for observing and understanding students. This frame of reference will make it possible to plan curriculum around specific learning preferences. You can more wisely and effectively choose topics, group students, organize activities, and manage time, space, and materials. When you use AORO is unimportant. Use it when you feel comfortable with it.

The task of using an observation instrument to observe 30 busy 8-year-olds or 120 adolescents may seem a daunting idea—one that may discourage you from trying. I can ease the burden by assuring you it is not necessary to observe all your students. Instead, observe those five or six students you wish to better understand. Be reassured that you can do any of this work at your own pace and in your own fashion. There is no one best way for everyone, but there is a way that is best for you.

In using AORO, you have three purposes:

1. You are learning a valuable frame of reference.
2. You are acquiring knowledge about your students that will aid your curriculum planning.
3. You are gathering data on the students that can be recorded in their cumulative records to assist the teachers with whom they will work in the years to come. Extraversion and introversion, unlike the functions Sensing/Intuition (S/N) or Thinking/Feeling (T/F), are nearly always chosen early in life and remain stable over time.

Observe, Don't Guess

AORO is a systematic observation instrument, which means you record what you see. It is unnecessary to evaluate what you record. The items on AORO describe behaviors you may observe as being action-oriented or reflection-oriented. Each item is designed to be *as low inference as possible*. That is to say, the descriptions of behavior are as precise and nonevaluative as the behavior allows. *However, you will have to make some inferences.* You will have to be familiar enough with the students, for example, to differentiate between a depressed action-oriented child and an excited reflection-oriented child.

Warning: A Natural Tendency

It's natural to assume that someone who behaves a certain way in one situation will behave the same way again. It's also natural to remember one incident in which, for example, a student was active and boisterous and from that one incident assume the child is action-oriented. To avoid this natural danger in using an observation instrument, you must check *only the behavior you actually observe* each observation period. This method is the vital characteristic of a sign system such as AORO.

When you are noting behaviors on the AORO form, you need make *only one checkmark* for each observed behavior. If a student is observed behaving once or twice in an "Outspoken" way (Item 18, Action-Oriented), you would check the "mildly evident" square. If, however, this student had often behaved in an outspoken way, you would check the "very evident" column *once*.

Check only the behaviors you actually see. It's quite unlikely that you will ever observe every behavior on the list during one observation period.

When to Observe Students

The instrument can be scored in the manner you feel is best for you to manage. It is a demanding task to teach and observe simultaneously. For that reason, the instrument is flexible, with no time requirements and no set number of students to be observed. It does not matter how many students you decide to observe and score at one time. As your familiarity with the instrument and with students increases, so will your ease and efficiency of observation.

Here are some ideas for observation:

1. Observe one student per period and score the instrument during the break.

The Introverted Learner ■ **E**xtraversion

19   ■ **I**ntroversion

■ **S**ensing

■ i**N**tuition

■ **T**hinking

■ **F**eeling

■ **J**udging

■ **P**erceiving

2. Observe and score students as another teacher (art, music, physical education, and so forth) carries the major teaching responsibility.

3. Observe several students each day, checking off observations during any available moments.

4. Observe several students while they are busy at different assigned tasks.

5. Inform the students that the teacher is busy learning about them and needs time to fill in some papers each day.

Student Choice

To observe students' preferred patterns of learning, you must observe during a period when students have some degree of choice. If students are functioning in a closely structured setting, you may be observing teacher preferences rather than student preferences. It is natural, too, for teachers to organize the world in the way they prefer. The ideal is to have the classroom operating in such a way that all members of the group function at their optimal levels of efficiency. Awareness of these optimal levels helps make that possible.

It Gets Easier

The initial period of observation is a training period in which the teacher learns to perceive in an empathic, systematic way, taking into account a very particular difference in the way another human being deals with the world.

Many teachers find that after this initial period (observing about five students, five times each), they begin to automatically focus attention in this fashion and use AORO to spot

check or to scientifically and objectively check out their perceptions.

Scoring AORO

Every child will display some characteristics in each category. This is normal. Scores will indicate the preferred way of tuning in to the world. To score AORO, simply add up the checks. "Mildly Evident" receives a score of one. "Very Evident" receives a score of two. "Not Evident" receives a score of zero. The category (that is, Action-Oriented or Reflection-Oriented) with the highest score determines the student's preference.

Because situations often influence behavior, it is a good idea to record the situation (math lesson, field trip, independent study) under which the student is being observed. Observe each student at least five times before making a final decision about whether action orientation or reflection orientation is truly the student's preferred pattern of learning.

Sharing Results

You may choose to share your observations with your students. Many students understand the concept of learning style. There is no evaluative connotation of good or better or smarter involved, and students come to appreciate the concern and expertise of their teacher. Awareness of the way one tunes into the world is very helpful to the young person in understanding why some tasks are particularly difficult or annoying while others are pleasant and easy.

Harvey Gilden felt comfortable with these instructions. He was ready to begin observing using AORO.

AORO Form: Action-Oriented

Student's Name_____Teacher's Name_____

Present Situation_____

I. Student prefers to act, then to think, and learns by doing.

Not Evident	Mildly Evident	Very Evident	Do you see the student
◯	◯	◯	1. Acting quickly?
◯	◯	◯	2. Moving from object to object or from person to person?
◯	◯	◯	3. Being impatient with delay?
◯	◯	◯	4. Asking questions about things happening now?
◯	◯	◯	5. Showing excitement about activities involving action?
◯	◯	◯	6. Choosing to use trial and error?
◯	◯	◯	7. Having a short attention span?
◯	◯	◯	8. Showing impatience with long, slow jobs?
◯	◯	◯	9. Expressing dislike of complicated procedures?
◯	◯	◯	10. Expressing a need to experience something in order to understand it?
◯	◯	◯	11. Sometimes taking on too many activities?

II. Student prefers to work with other people and learns by interacting.

Not Evident	Mildly Evident	Very Evident	Do you see the student
◯	◯	◯	12. Choosing to work with others?
◯	◯	◯	13. Asking what other people are doing?
◯	◯	◯	14. Talking frequently with the teacher?
◯	◯	◯	15. Asking how others solve problems?
◯	◯	◯	16. Eagerly attending to interruptions?
◯	◯	◯	17. Readily offering opinions?
◯	◯	◯	18. Talking over new ideas with other people?
◯	◯	◯	19. Appearing friendly and congenial?
◯	◯	◯	20. Appearing confident and relaxed?

■ **E**xtraversion
■ **I**ntroversion
■ **S**ensing
■ i**N**tuition
■ **T**hinking
■ **F**eeling
■ **J**udging
■ **P**erceiving

AORO Form: Action-Oriented (*continued*)

Student's Name_____Teacher's Name_____

Present Situation_____

III. Student prefers to work orally and learns by talking.

Not Evident	Mildly Evident	Very Evident	Do you see the student
○	○	○	21. Being outspoken?
○	○	○	22. Being talkative?
○	○	○	23. Agreeing to give spontaneous speeches?
○	○	○	24. Sharing personal experiences?
○	○	○	25. Communicating well?
○	○	○	26. Being good at greeting people?
○	○	○	27. Adding new ideas when talking about an issue?

IV. Student prefers an external source of motivation.

Not Evident	Mildly Evident	Very Evident	Do you see the student
○	○	○	28. Asking the teacher for feedback on tasks being performed?
○	○	○	29. Asking questions to check out group expectations?
○	○	○	30. Choosing topics or assignments that have value to other people?
○	○	○	31. Expressing satisfaction over pleasing others?

AORO Form: Reflection-Oriented

Student's Name_____Teacher's Name_____

Present Situation_____

I. Student prefers to think, then to act, and learns by thinking, then doing.

Not Evident	Mildly Evident	Very Evident	Do you see the student
○	○	○	1. Appearing to be deep in thought?
○	○	○	2. Taking time to think before acting?
○	○	○	3. Holding back from new experiences?
○	○	○	4. Pausing before answering?
○	○	○	5. Being uncomfortable with spontaneous questioning?
○	○	○	6. Searching for facts to confirm ideas?
○	○	○	7. Asking questions to allow understanding something before attempting to do it?
○	○	○	8. Sticking to complicated tasks?
○	○	○	9. Having a long attention span?

II. Student prefers to work alone and learns on own.

Not Evident	Mildly Evident	Very Evident	Do you see the student
○	○	○	10. Choosing to work alone or with one person?
○	○	○	11. Asking for a quiet space to work?
○	○	○	12. Showing annoyance at being interrupted?
○	○	○	13. Being reluctant to give personal information?
○	○	○	14. Carefully selecting a few friends?
○	○	○	15. Appearing shy?
○	○	○	16. Bottling up emotion?

■ **E**xtraversion
■ **I**ntroversion
■ **S**ensing
■ i**N**tuition
■ **T**hinking
■ **F**eeling
■ **J**udging
■ **P**erceiving

AORO Form: Reflection-Oriented (*continued*)

Student's Name_____Teacher's Name_____

Present Situation_____

III. Student prefers nonverbal learning and does best work in head.

Not Evident	Mildly Evident	Very Evident	Do you see the student
○	○	○	17. Being quiet?
○	○	○	18. Enjoying library projects?
○	○	○	19. Choosing a written assignment over oral presentation?
○	○	○	20. Entering carefully and slowly into discussions?
○	○	○	21. Having problems communicating orally?
○	○	○	22. Enjoying reading assignments?
○	○	○	23. Reading for pleasure or escape?
○	○	○	24. Performing better in written work than in oral presentations?

IV. Student prefers own internal source of motivation.

Not Evident	Mildly Evident	Very Evident	Do you see the student
○	○	○	25. Working intently on task at hand?
○	○	○	26. Working on one thing for a long time?
○	○	○	27. Making own decisions?
○	○	○	28. Becoming frustrated when things cannot be done the way pupil feels they should?
○	○	○	29. Setting own standards when possible?
○	○	○	30. Seeming hard to understand?
○	○	○	31. Being willing to pursue something independently without group or teacher approval?

Applying Knowledge in the Classroom

Finally Harvey was ready to apply his knowledge to classroom practice. He studied and carefully followed the suggestions given in the *AORO Manual* (excerpted here):

General Applications for Learning

Some practical examples of taking into account theoretical and clinical descriptions of *extraverted, action orientation* would be:

1. Group students so that they may discuss issues of importance. (Extraverts learn as they interact talking about a topic.)

2. Create an atmosphere in which it is safe to make mistakes. (Extraverts learn by trial and error.)

3. Set up learning centers in which students can move about from project to project. (Extraverts have a shorter attention span, enjoy variety, and need to be able to physically move about in the classroom.)

4. Provide opportunities for students to be evaluated orally or in a practical way. (Extraverts do well in verbal transactions and are very practical in orientation.)

5. Be patient and encouraging when giving directions, providing guidelines, and in allowing students to study one another's work. (Extraverts prefer an external source of motivation and derive great pleasure from pleasing others.)

6. Give precise, patient guidance in having students work alone on completing a long or complex project. (Solitude is especially difficult for an extravert.)

In planning for *introverted, reflective-oriented* students, the teacher could:

1. Take precautions in questioning the class, extending wait time after a question is asked, writing questions on the board before questioning begins, having students write down their answers to questions before giving them orally. (Introverts need time to reflect before answering. Note: Because extraverts generally don't need as much wait time, they usually tend to dominate the question-answer phase of learning.)

2. Have a space (such as a carrel) available in the classroom in which students can isolate themselves when they feel a need. (Introverts hate interruptions when working, need to be private in their own territory to complete tasks or to "charge up their batteries" before they enjoy interaction.)

3. Team students who have similar interests. (Introverts work well in pairs or small groups, especially with people whom they trust and/or with whom they share a common interest.)

4. Be patient when some students tend not to open up emotionally, appear difficult to understand, or have little regard for external sources of motivation. (Privacy is natural to the introvert).

5. Allow plenty of preparation time and choice in making oral presentations. (Only when the introvert is given time and opportunity to share a subject she knows and loves does she enjoy sharing with an audience.)

6. Provide opportunity for students to read for pleasure or escape to

■ **E**xtraversion

■ **I**ntroversion

■ **S**ensing

■ i**N**tuition

■ **T**hinking

■ **F**eeling

■ **J**udging

■ **P**erceiving

a quiet space or the library to complete written assignments or projects. (The introvert enjoys and excels in self-directed, focused projects).

This process of observing gave Harvey Gilden the time, opportunity, and sense of security he needed before he could seriously consider using any of these ideas in his classroom. Both Anna and Harvey, teachers in the same school, are learning about type theory, but they will go about applying it in the classroom in very different ways. This is how it should be. A program that promotes differences in students must honor and respect individual differences in teachers.

3

The Sensing Learner

▶ What is sensation?

The perceiving function that seeks immediately relevant and accessible experience through the senses.

▶ How does sensation affect behavior?

It causes the person to pay careful attention to each detail in his immediate environment in a practical, focused way.

▶ How does sensation affect the way one interacts, communicates, and teaches?

It causes the person to appreciate and enjoy traditional, familiar surroundings and to deal with the world in a realistic, down-to-earth manner. The sensing teacher teaches uses a straightforward developmental system, moving students carefully from one

The Sensing Learner

27

- **E**xtraversion
- **I**ntroversion
- **S**ensing
- i**N**tuition
- **T**hinking
- **F**eeling
- **J**udging
- **P**erceiving

level of learning to the next. The teacher's fundamentally practical approach allows most students to recognize the purpose motivating their learning. This teacher likes to feel she serves the school well.

▶ How does a preference for sensation translate into learning style?

1. Sensing students move cautiously into new learning, prefer a set procedure, and usually learn one step at a time. They like to stick to skills and knowledge they already possess and learn best by building on those in a developmental learning mode.

2. Sensing students dislike abstract theory and tend to skip over theory when it is presented to them. This omission often makes them feel guilty, stupid, or resentful. Theory must be presented in small pieces, as it relates to the immediate learning task, and only when absolutely necessary. Sensing types need to see a practical reason and immediate payoff for learning.

3. Sensing students are like open sponges, absorbing information through all the senses. They want to see, hear, and touch as they learn. Often, they can learn by observing and mimicking behaviors. Such students learn very quickly when they can look over a step-by-step procedure, see it performed, then try it themselves.

Sensing types distrust most forms of evaluation other than the simple question "Can they do the task?" Essay questions, formal test situations, and aptitude tests put sensing students at a disadvantage, and often they do not perform well in these situations. It is a pity when such students are forced to take those tests because they serve no useful function for the students.

Nor are they indicative of what the sensing students really know or can perform.

▶ How does the teacher respond to these preferences?

The teacher designs the program by breaking it down into the component parts. She proceeds slowly and allows students plenty of time for observation and practice.

The teacher needs to create the opportunity to discover for herself the sensing students' level of skill and knowledge. Learning should often include some things the sensing students already know, thus laying the foundation for success at the next level.

The teacher provides plenty of opportunity for hands-on, practical, nontheoretical learning. Any theory must be relevant and serve a practical purpose. Learning for learning's sake should be avoided.

Close-up: Sensing

Vicki Wynn had taught 3rd grade for 17 years. She enjoyed the familiar routine. Then came the big change. She was promoted to the position of vice-principal, which included the responsibility of teaching half-time in a 6th grade class.

To prepare herself for her new position, Vicki attended the University at Stanford for a summer course in educational methods. She felt a real need to familiarize herself with some of the recent methods and philosophies of education. In the course, Vicki learned about the Jungian approach to learning styles. She found the method wonderfully systematic and precise.

Vicki completed the Myers-Briggs Type Indicator and found out she was an ISFJ—an Introverted, Sensing Feeling, Judging type—whose favorite function was sensa-

tion. As a sensing type, Vicki was pleased with all the factual material available to her. Her summer months as a student were happy ones. She worked hard, made good grades, and came to her new job in the fall armed with a lot of practical information. Although she had some worries about being able to meet the needs of intuitive types, she felt strong and determined.

Within a few weeks, however, Vicki's sense of security and happiness was quickly replaced by feelings of harried anxiety. Her duties as vice-principal and her new job in an unfamiliar grade put such demands on her time and so taxed her resources that she just couldn't imagine herself designing curriculum for 16 different types of students. She almost wished she hadn't gone to summer school or learned about type theory. Now she had to live with a feeling that she wasn't doing all she could and should be doing.

She was reluctant to start applying her new knowledge until she had a good chunk of time. She had learned enough in summer school to know that designing curriculum for all types took a lot of thought.

Her professor had divided the class into four groups:

- EN (extraversion, intuition)
- IN (introversion, intuition)
- ES (extraversion sensing)
- IS (introversion, sensing)

The learning style preferences experienced by these groups, he said, were the most important in developing curriculum. The professor asked each group to come up with a description of their preferred learning style and present it to the group. That part was easy. For instance, this is how the ENs described their learning style:

The Sensing Learner

29

■ **E**xtraversion
■ **I**ntroversion
■ **S**ensing
■ i**N**tuition
■ **T**hinking
■ **F**eeling
■ **J**udging
■ **P**erceiving

EN's LEARNING PREFERENCES

• make it relevant, have personal meaning
• let us play with it, invent it
• it must involve some social interaction
• let us know how and why—let us figure it out on our own
• cause an adrenalin rush
• give us choices
• give us as few instructions as possible
• we like to be mobile and visible
• expect us to be non-sequential
• never test for facts—let us use facts to develop concepts
• relax—we'll get it
• give us deadlines
• include us in whole process including evaluation

Then the professor had Vicki and her classmates design curriculum for each group. They struggled all of one afternoon. This is how the IN group planned a lesson for the EN group:

LESSON PLAN FOR EN

Develop a text that explains how the continental drift occurs

• break into small brainstorming group
• elect someone to be a scribe
• discuss your collective knowledge
• come up with an explanation for the continental drift
• you may use library, telephone
• you have 1/2 hour in class time
• there will be a debrief of the topic and teacher will record your ideas
• you may choose to work further on the topic if you wish to check with experts

---

The ENs applauded the INs. Then the IS group presented their ideas. The IS group had chosen to teach dinosaurs. This is how they interpreted the EN type's need

to work collectively, to have degrees of freedom, and to be creative:

| **IS** | Curriculum for ENs |

1. Examine these categories
   a. Size
   b. Food
   c. Habitat
2. Fill in the blanks
3. Group/individual—go to library
4. Draw pictures or tell stories

There was an uncomfortable pause. The EN group didn't know what to say. The IS group figured they had done something wrong. They asked the ENs to show them what they would have preferred. In minutes, the ENs came up with this idea:

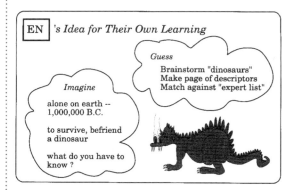

The IS group was stunned by their misinterpretation of the EN group's preferences.

The professor then turned the tables and asked all the groups to develop curriculum for the IS group, who described their learning preferences like this:

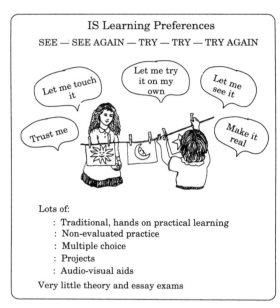

IS Learning Preferences

SEE — SEE AGAIN — TRY — TRY — TRY AGAIN

Let me touch it

Let me try it on my own

Let me see it

Trust me

Make it real

Lots of:
: Traditional, hands on practical learning
: Non-evaluated practice
: Multiple choice
: Projects
: Audio-visual aids
Very little theory and essay exams

SOURCE: ZEISSET 1985

This time it was the EN group's turn to squirm. In response to the IS need for observation, specifics, and practical application, the EN group came up with this lesson plan for studying frogs:

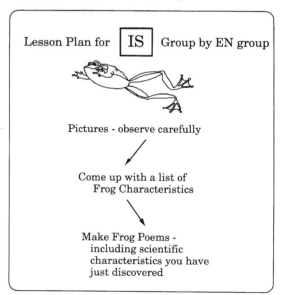

Lesson Plan for IS Group by EN group

Pictures - observe carefully

Come up with a list of Frog Characteristics

Make Frog Poems - including scientific characteristics you have just discovered

The IS group roared with laughter. They were all learning how difficult it is to understand what their opposite types mean when they explain their needs. It is natural for types to interpret those needs based on their own preferences, which of course bias their understanding.

The IS group explained that writing frog poems containing scientific characteristics was an N idea of working with specifics in practical, real ways. The IS group came up with their own plan for learning about frogs:

IS Lesson Plan for Themselves

1. Watch film
2. Examine sheet of listed facts
3. Examine pictures of different kinds
4. Field trip
5. Multiple choice exam

Each group learned that it's easy to design curriculum for your own learning style group, fairly easy to design it for those folks with whom you share some preferences, but difficult to design tasks for your opposite type. This is especially true for sensing types who are designing curriculum for intuitives.

When Vicki remembered this exercise and how hard they had all worked at understanding one another, she felt depressed. How could she possibly do this right when she was so busy?

Vicki need not have been so hard on herself. No teacher working in today's demanding school system has time to create 16 different curricula over and over again. First of all, most of Vicki's students

The Sensing Learner

31

- ■ **E**xtraversion
- ■ **I**ntroversion
- ■ **S**ensing
- ■ i**N**tuition
- ■ **T**hinking
- ■ **F**eeling
- ■ **J**udging
- ■ **P**erceiving

are sensing types. Therefore she will naturally develop curriculum in a way that meets their needs. Furthermore, the intuitives in the class will love the challenge of designing curriculum for themselves; of course, the teacher must guide them by providing expectations, evaluations, criteria, and due dates. They will benefit from, value, and appreciate this opportunity.

There are several options for the cautious sensing teacher to use besides giving the students choices in designing assignments or suggesting ways they would like to go about learning something. Another strategy, probably more comfortable for the sensing teacher, would be to make a list of the eight preferences (E, I and S, N and T, F and J, P), and to systematically work through a unit making sure that at *some* time, all eight preferences are covered. As Vicki discovered in summer school, it is natural for a teacher to use methods that suit her own learning style. In Vicki's case that would be in an ISFJ style. Making a list and working through it systematically would assure that no types would be disadvantaged.

Another strategy would be to team teach with a person whose type is different from the teacher's own. A group of three teachers of ISFJ, ESTP, and INFJ types, for example, can cover all types and naturally assure a variety of teaching and learning styles. If teachers do not actually team teach, they might "team design"—that is, they might help one another by exchanging units and asking for suggestions of ways to fill in type gaps.

Team efforts relieve individual teachers of the huge responsibility of developing curriculum for all types; they also provide a wonderful opportunity for teachers to work together in a practical, purposeful, and collegial way. Teaching can be a lonely profession. Most teachers welcome productive, uncontrived, time-saving ways of working together.

RESOURCES

To learn more about developing curriculum for different types, see *People Types and Tiger Stripes*, 2nd ed., by Gordon Lawrence (Gainesville, Fla.: Center for Applications of Psychological Type, 1982).

4

The Intuitive Learner

▶ What is intuition?

The perceiving function that makes sense of the world by creating patterns and inventing hypotheses.

▶ How does intuition affect behavior?

It causes the person to scan situations and data in order to see relationships between things in a way that is self-inspiring and inventive.

▶ How does intuition affect the way one interacts, communicates, and teaches?

It causes the person to crave intense experiences, full of change and adventure and innovation. Motivated by inspiration and idealism, intuitive teachers are driven by visions of how education should be and how the classroom might be. Intuitive

The Intuitive Learner

33

■ **E**xtraversion
■ **I**ntroversion
■ **S**ensing
■ **iN**tuition
■ **T**hinking
■ **F**eeling
■ **J**udging
■ **P**erceiving

teachers enjoy the challenge of big projects and new experiences and, thus, they push students to challenge themselves. They push them to grow, experience, and discover. Rarely guided by curriculum outlines, intuitive teachers create their own curriculum and are confident that they will cover the essentials—and more.

▶ How does a preference for intuition translate into learning style?

1. Intuitive students are inventive learners who like to make up possible hypotheses, explanations, and ways of doing things, as they go along. They would rather guess first and be told later, as a checkpoint. They enjoy adding their own original touch or idea to any given situation and will put more energy into a project when they are encouraged to invent and take risks.

2. Intuitive students get bored easily and seek variety in how and what they learn. They dislike repetition and resent it deeply when the teacher forces them into a review situation. If intuitive students must review, they do it best by testing wits or teaching their peers.

3. Intuitive students work unevenly and grow in spurts and starts. At the start of a project, their energy is often focused and intense. Then their attention may lapse, but it generally returns to an intense level by the end of the project. Intuitive students tend to skip over what they consider unimportant details and often get them wrong or forget them. Intuitive students pay attention to details only if they serve their larger purpose, such as supporting a hypothesis in a report or an experimental study.

▶ How does the teacher respond to these preferences?

The teacher designs a variety of programs that provide intuitive students with plenty of opportunities to invent, guess, teach, and work independently beyond the scope of the program.

He sets up opportunities for independent learning where the intuitive students will have access to experts and additional knowledge when they want it.

Close-up: Intuition

Mary Higgins teaches in the Milbery Middle School. It is her fifth year in the school. She enjoys teaching, but finds herself secretly longing to teach creative writing in a senior high school. She has been writing, and reading about writing, and taking night courses in writing. In short, she has been bitten by the writing bug. As a result, she has showered her 5th and 6th grade classes with activities that have grown out of her enthusiasm.

Even though Mary is applying everything she's learning to making her new writing program work, most of her students are not responding the way she expected they would. What could be wrong? Don't they want to write their own stories? Don't they like what she's doing? Mary feels strangely betrayed.

What Mary doesn't know is that most of her students prefer sensing as a way of interpreting the world (70 percent prefer sensation, 30 percent prefer intuition). Mary is an intuitive type, and she teaches in the style natural to her. She reads her favorite poems or short stories aloud to inspire students. She tells them to write about the things they know and care about. She believes in variety and choices, and she creates high energy and excitement in the classroom to stimulate students into writing interesting and imaginative stories. Inspired by her own intuition, Mary seeks intuitive ways of doing things to inspire others. And, like other intuitive teachers, she is deeply troubled when the methods she finds so exciting fail to produce the same response in others.

Mary can have "intuitive challenges" that excite her sensing students if she channels her enthusiasm and knowledge into sensing modes of operating. But she doesn't know how. And so she struggles, swimming against the current, getting a few of her students to write great poems, while others write mundane descriptions that lack

the power she'd hoped for. Too much of the student writing lacks direction and emotional impact.

Mary tries another tactic. She yearns for her students to expand their work, to take a bit of truth and let it grow, to explore places of imagination and creativity. But how? She tells them to write about a time they almost got lost. "Pretend you actually did get lost, let me see how it felt," she says. Her students write three sentences. *I was scared. I cried. A policeman found me.* Mary is even more discouraged.

Her instincts have told her that using prose models is useful. She reads Willa Cather's "Paul's Case" to her class. They love the story. She feels encouraged. She writes in big letters on the board. "Imagine what would have happened to Paul if he had committed suicide. Write a new ending to Willa Cather's book. It might help if you imagined yourself as Paul. Write your own story."

Once again, she is terribly disappointed by the fact that many of her students write only a few lines. Most are not inspired. Some even shrug, commenting that Willa Cather killed Paul off, and after all, dead is dead, why would they write a new ending? Some try hard to write a new ending. They like their teacher and want to please her. But they simply don't know where to begin. It seems such a silly task, and they could make up anything.

Thank goodness a few of the students do get it. They make up wonderful endings showing real understanding of the issues involved and the characters created by Willa Cather. Mary reads those stories out loud. But reading the "good" answers doesn't seem to inspire or instruct the other students.

What Mary hasn't yet learned is that she must use the writing models in very precise

The Intuitive Learner

35

■ **E**xtraversion
■ **I**ntroversion
■ **S**ensing
■ i**N**tuition
■ **T**hinking
■ **F**eeling
■ **J**udging
■ **P**erceiving

ways. The task she has assigned has no validity for most of her students. The assignment is loose and ungrounded. The students can't understand why their teacher gets so excited about these "nonsense" assignments. The value of one is the nonvalue of the other, theorizes Jung. And in this case, he is absolutely right. What excites Mary only confuses or frightens or bores most of her students.

The problem is that only the intuitive students are getting it. Mary's question, "What would happen if Paul had not committed suicide," is a highly intuitive one. The sensing students are unsure how to use their intuition. If you ask a sensing child to perform an intuitive task, you must first engage the sensing function. When teaching students type, it is essential to use the function they naturally prefer as part of the whole process. But Mary Higgins hasn't yet learned how to do this. She doesn't yet know "type talk." But she will soon. The topic of her next writing workshop is "Jung and His Archetypes: How to Use Type Theory to Create Convincing Characters."

At the writing workshop, bells ring for Mary. In true intuitive leaping, she hears her professor explain about creating real characters, and she transfers that information to understanding her students. (One of the great joys of intuitive learning is that all knowledge is relevant in one way or another.) The professor explains that most people in everyday life are sensing types. "Write in a lot of sensing characters," he suggests. "Sensing types like to go from the known to the unknown carefully. They don't like to jump in. They like to know the rules. Remember these things when you create your standard character," the professor says.

Mary returns to her classroom charged with new energy and purpose. She has discovered sensing types and what they are like. She has accidentally discovered the world of learning styles by translating character traits to learning traits.

From the list of descriptors she received in her writing class, she realizes that she must identify forms or structures for her sensing students to use. "Write a poem in blank verse about anything you care about" has not been very helpful for the sensing students. They want to follow the rules of a haiku, a diamond poem, or a metaphor poem. For the sensing students, poetry writing requires structure as a starting point. The writing needs a topic and a purpose. Then the words will come. The golden rule for Mary becomes "Structure frees." She is amazed at the work that begins to appear. Her walls are plastered with examples of great writing. Everyone is engaged. She has combined her knowledge of writing with her knowledge of how students learn best. It is a winning combination.

Mary offers those students who received low marks in the "Paul's Case" assignment the opportunity to try again. For those with high grades, she suggests they design several skits and plan a celebration day for everyone to be held at the end of the week. "Conquering Willa Cather" they will call it. Her intuitive students love the challenge and the freedom.

As the intuitive students work on their own, Mary can focus on teaching "Paul's Case" to her sensing students. She walks them through a realistic process. The first stage in the process is to let them believe that Paul is not dead. She has her students imagine that Paul jumps in front of the train, as Willa Cather wrote it. But Paul is small, he is afraid. He huddles in fear against the ground and the train rides right over him without touching him. Too frightened to try again, he must face life. What does he do?

Now that the students are ready to believe Paul is alive, Mary teaches them about making intuitive leaps. She explains that intuition relies on facts, even if it doesn't know it. Sensing types love facts. They love to and are able to write great lists of facts about Paul. They are instructed to write down everything they know about him—his stealing the money, his being imaginative, his loving the theater, his feeling different, and so forth.

Next Mary asks her students to circle all the things that they have written about Paul that would help them to make an educated guess about what Paul would do if he hadn't died under the train. The sensing students can then "fill in the blanks," which is another favorite task. Paul might . . . or he might . . . because . . . (what follows are all the facts they circled from their list of Paul facts). Mary tells them, "Elaborate. Turn your sentence into a story."

Now the sensing students are ready to intuit, to hypothesize, to create and invent. Through the path of sensation, they have found intuition and have something concrete on which to base their stories. They are ready to play "let's pretend."

As Mary learns more about type theory, she applies what she knows to her new knowledge about writing. She discovers that writing is a wonderful way to help intuitive students practice their sensation and to help sensing types practice their intuition. Good writing comprises generalities, universal truths, and specific facts. Sensation serves intuition in that it provides the details that dramatize and make par-

ticular the person, place, and time of the story. Intuition serves sensation in that it provides the underlying universal elements within the big picture of the story.

Mary focuses on sensation and intuition for the rest of the year. She has made a wise choice because so much of learning style is determined by sensation and intuition. Simply focusing on how to help her sensing students (who compose 70 percent of the classroom) to use sensation to do the intuitive task of writing and reading, of hypothesizing and thinking about larger issues, is a worthwhile goal for the year. And her intuitive students will appreciate learning the writing trick of using specifics, details, and concrete images to make their stories come alive.

The study of sensation and intuition is complex and suits Mary's intuitive nature, which exults in discovering the relationships that exist between various aspects of curriculum and student preferences.

As Mary develops her skills in this area of type theory, she learns a lot about giving choices and finding alternative methods. She discovers a way to get into the heads of her students so she can present materials and talk in ways that appeal to them. Mary forgets all about wanting to move to Smart Student High.

Intuitive teachers often love finding ways to take their intuitive imaginations and work in realistic, practical ways that appeal to sensing students. The process is challenging and rewarding.

RESOURCES

There are many books available to help the teacher learn more about sensing types. A good place to start is *LIFETypes* by S. Hirsh and J. Kummerow (New York: Warner Books, 1989).

5

The Thinking Learner

▶ What is thinking?

It is the judgment function that values objective, analytical ways to make decisions and evaluate situations.

How does thinking affect behavior?

It causes the person to stand back, remaining cool and a bit aloof so that she can think logically and rationally, honestly and fairly, and, if necessary, critically.

▶ How does thinking affect the way one interacts, communicates, and teaches?

It causes the person to value an objective, fair world that runs on logical principles. The thinking teacher will present the goals and objectives of learning to the class; she always wants truth, fairness, and an equal chance to meet expectations to be available to all students. If students do not meet the outlined objectives, the thinking teacher will criticize objectively, readily, and often publicly, making sure the students know where they stand and realize where they are failing to meet thé standards set by the thinker. The thinking teacher is task-oriented and can ignore students' feelings if she is not convinced that it is important to include personal, emotional issues in the equation for successful teaching.

▶ How does a preference for thinking translate into learning style?

1. Thinking students value honesty and fair play and deeply resent any signs of favoritism. They believe rules should be followed to the letter.

2. Thinking students can be competitive, driven, independent learners—demanding of themselves and others. They like to win and to always appear confident. If thinkers are made to feel incompetent in front of others, they may become so distressed that they mentally withdraw from the classroom.

3. Thinking students need well-organized, logically developed courses of study. They value, respect, and expect expert knowledge.

▶ How does the teacher respond to these preferences?

The teacher designs well-organized programs with cause-and-effect sequences clearly evident.

She is careful to respect the thinkers' need for competence and offers every opportunity to succeed, protecting thinkers from failure or ridicule.

She offers thinking students the opportunity to compete in healthy ways, particularly with themselves rather than others. Thinkers are recognized for their excellence.

Close-up: Thinking

Chris Iannella wasn't very pleased when he read the description of his ENTJ type. He objected to being described as "seemingly aloof or even indifferent, especially to feeling types."

Aloof? Indifferent? The school board had asked Chris to complete the Myers-Briggs Type Inventory and he had, in good faith. Now this. It was insulting! And frightening. Would they judge him negatively? Were they already judging him? Was this why he had been asked to complete the MBTI? Could it be true that people thought

The Thinking Learner

39

■ **E**xtraversion
■ **I**ntroversion
■ **S**ensing
■ i**N**tuition
■ **T**hinking
■ **F**eeling
■ **J**udging
■ **P**erceiving

him indifferent? The possibility made him so mad he felt sick to his stomach.

Chris never felt indifferent about anything. He was considered a tough but fair teacher. Strict, yes, demanding of his students, yes. But never indifferent. Surely the reason he was so strict, so demanding, was that he cared so much.

His type description also said he seemed overly critical and so concerned about getting things done that he could hurt people's feelings in the process. This criticism made Chris even more uncomfortable. He was a bit on the critical side, he knew. But that wasn't because he didn't care about kids. It was because he did care. He wanted them to understand their math, their history, their geography, everything.

Could it be that he was a bit too strict? Maybe he should have stuck to teaching college math, but the public schools needed strong teachers to give young students a good start. That was why he left his much easier college position for the challenge of teaching elementary school. That night, Chris's mind raced with worried thoughts.

In the morning Chris headed for the library. He read all weekend. He focused his reading on understanding the Jungian notions of thinking and feeling that seemed to be the source of his trouble. As he read, he began to relax and things began to make sense. The one idea that really jumped out at him was the Jungian explanation of criticism: Basically, thinking types offer criticism out of a sense of duty and caring. They want to help fix the problem. Critical analysis is one of their favorite tools in problem solving. The feeling types, however, don't want the problem solved; they want the problem *understood*. The thinkers stand back and analyze; the feelers jump in and empathize.

THINKING	FEELING
Tendencies/Characteristics	Tendencies/Characteristics
Sees things as on-looker, from outside a situation.	Sees things as a participant, from within a situation
Takes a long view.	Takes an immediate and personal view
Spontaneously finds flaws, criticizes.	Spontaneously appreciates.

SOURCE: Earle C. Page, *Looking at Type*, 2nd ed. (Gainesville, Fla.: Center for Applications of Psychological Type, 1992). © 1992 CAPT.

Chris felt guilty. How many times had his school principal asked him not to try to fix everything? And how Chris had been confused, and even hurt, by her rejection of his help.

Chris decided to discuss his anxieties with his wife. He could trust her with these feelings. It was a good talk, though not easy. His wife admitted that she, too, would sometimes prefer that he show some sympathetic understanding rather than try to fix things for her. Often this tendency made her feel inadequate, uncared for— "even though I know you secretly love me," she had added with a wink.

They laughed over that, but Chris was getting some hard lessons in dealing with feeling types, especially in the way one goes about dealing with them when they feel they have made a mistake.

"I usually know all the things I've done wrong," explained his wife. "What I really need is for you to listen. Maybe make a cup of tea?"

A cup of tea! Not a brilliant solution? A cup of tea would be a lot easier, that was for sure. Chris knew his wife respected him and valued his advice. Even before this talk, he had sensed that she was more grateful for his help when she asked for it than when he'd foisted it on her.

But his students. That was different. It was his job to help them and give them his advice. He was their teacher.

Chris headed back to the books and articles on type theory. He trusted knowledge. He instinctively felt he just needed to know more. In one article he read the following advice: "It is the job of the teacher to remain accepting of the ways of others while deciding how best to interfere" (Mamchur 1994, p. 101). Chris laughed out loud. He read the advice again. He certainly agreed on the interference part. And he was good at it. His students learned. Education is, after all, about change. And his students did change! "Remain accepting." Now that was the part that sometimes eluded Chris. He believed in this concept in principle, but often took for granted that his students knew he accepted them.

Chris was a fair man, an honest man. He recognized a weakness in his approach. He decided to try more consciously to take into account the "feeling" aspect of teaching. He would focus on empathy and acceptance. He decided, for the first time, that there was actually a systematic way for him to attend to this rather difficult area. He decided that type theory might be a useful tool, not a threat to his livelihood and self-esteem.

Thinking types are the most likely to reject or be upset by some aspects of their type description. This reaction could be based on a combination of things. First, Isabel Myers was a dominantly feeling type and, even as aware as she was of type strengths, she may have used language that set a harsh tone in describing thinking.

In addition, thinking types are very sensitive to any criticism that might make them look incompetent. They may feel guilty and defensive about any accusation of being too critical or unfeeling or demanding. Often they've heard this criticism many times.

Type theory can help others understand and accept the thinking type by allowing them to recognize the true motive and genuine caring behind the thinker's actions. Even more important, type theory can provide thinking types with a systematic way to develop strategies for dealing with their own underdeveloped feeling function and for dealing with feeling types.

Usually, this learning process isn't easy. It takes time, perseverance, and courage. Chris was a busy man. He had spent weeks reading and thinking and talking about "this feeling and thinking business." He'd spent the whole Easter break coming to terms with this part of his life. But when he was finished, he walked into his classroom feeling a lot better, a lot stronger, and a lot better equipped "to remain accepting of the ways of others while trying to decide how best to interfere."

RESOURCES

Teachers who want to learn more about basic type theory may want to read *Gifts Differing: Understanding Personality Type* by Isabel Briggs Myers with Peter B. Myers (Palo Alto, Calif.: Davies-Black, 1995).

6

The Feeling Learner

▶ What is feeling?

it's good for me, it's good for you, it's good for us all!

The judging function that values subjective analysis and empathetic understanding as a means of decision making and evaluation.

▶ How does feeling affect behavior?

It causes the person to seek a personal and harmonious relationship with the environment, relying on a deep sense of personal values to guide behavior and judge the behavior of others.

▶ How does feeling affect the way one interacts, communicates, and teaches?

It causes the person to orient herself toward relationships, to attend to relating sympathetically with others in an attempt to create harmony in the world around her. The feeling teacher pays close attention to her personal values and to human needs in designing school programs. Guided by what she believes to be correct, and determined that others should live within clear rules of right and wrong, the feeling teacher can be insistent about the way things are done. Idealistic and principled, the feeling teacher will passionately strive to achieve personal goals and bring to fruition her personal vision of education.

▶ How does a preference for feeling translate into learning style?

1. Feeling students need a harmonious environment in which to learn. They take everything personally. The teacher must avoid harsh criticism. Even if criticism is not directed at feeling types, they feel uncomfortable when it is going on. Feeling students want a sense of decorum and respectful manners to prevail in the classroom.

2. Feeling students value cooperation, consideration, and consensus. They rarely appreciate competition because they believe that no one should be made to lose or feel second best. Feeling students like to please and are motivated by this desire in the classroom.

3. Feeling students want learning to help them grow in a personal way or to be more able to serve the world in the largest humanistic sense. Learning peaks for them when values are a motivating factor. Feeling students also learn best from an instructor whom they like as a person.

▶ How does the teacher respond to these preferences?

Above all, the teacher needs to be genuine and empathetic. This demands not only integrity but an open and honest interactive style that consistently demonstrates a match between spoken beliefs and actions.

The teacher needs to pay close attention to the learning environment, ensuring that it is pleasant and harmonious. She must never appear aloof or uncaring. Sarcasm is usually resented by feeling students.

The Feeling Learner

■ **E**xtraversion

■ **I**ntroversion

43

■ **S**ensing

■ i**N**tuition

■ **T**hinking

■ **F**eeling

■ **J**udging

■ **P**erceiving

The teacher must be constantly aware that feeling students respond in a personal way to everything that happens. It helps to make clear the value of the learning to the learner and the learner's world. When truly engaged, feeling students commit themselves to their work.

Close-up: Feeling

Verne Powers wasn't getting anywhere with his principal, Maggie Squash. She wasn't giving an inch. Verne couldn't understand it. He was so convinced that his ideas would work. Why couldn't he convince her?

Verne Powers, an INFP with a master's degree in English, and an IQ that leapt off the scale, had a passion for life and literature that made him the envy of his whole family, but he seemed to be surprisingly inept in getting his ideas off the ground in his own school.

Verne had been assigned what the other teachers affectionately called "the wild bunch," those students who, for a variety of reasons, had reached the 10th grade without having acquired one basic skill: literacy.

What they had acquired, however, were low self-esteem, truancy, and disruptive behavior.

While Verne was diligently trying the "mastery learning" methods and the "write to read" individualized computer programs the school had in place, his heart was elsewhere. He deeply believed that these students needed action and hands-on experience with the arts. He just knew that their path to learning to read lay in painting posters, putting on plays, and forming their own funky band. Expression, that's what it was all about: doing, playing, being a part of events and projects, finding a voice, and feeling the rush of success.

But these hands-on programs took time away from computers. They also required space and materials, were difficult to evaluate, and provided lots of opportunity for noise, disruption, and problems.

Though frustrated, Verne was not really surprised by the response he was getting from his principal. It had happened before in staff meetings. During a heated discussion, Verne would have a solution, a breakthrough idea. Full of passion and conviction, he would offer his solution, only to be ignored or even teased about his heated responses. Hours or sometimes weeks later, someone would come up with an idea similar to his original idea, and the "new" idea would be accepted, even hailed as a great solution.

It wasn't so much that Verne resented not getting credit for the idea, or that so much time was wasted in getting where he had been days before. It was that he wasn't taken seriously, wasn't, apparently, understood.

Verne is one of many young feeling types, particularly NFP feeling types, who are frustrated by their inability in some settings, usually at work, to be persuasive in making changes they believe in. The problem is frustrating for two reasons. First, feeling types, particularly NFs, are by nature change agents, longing to introduce positive and noble influences to the societies in which they live. Second, in many circumstances the feeling type is very persuasive, charismatic, even evangelistic. Passionate and energetic, this type can lead church groups, sports teams, and student unions. Why not a school principal? A staff of teachers?

Often the young feeling type has not yet learned the language of institutions, particularly the language used by the leaders of those institutions. STJ types are often represented in these settings. Research appearing in the *Myers-Briggs Type Indicator Atlas* indicates that more than half of 276 principals attending institute programs reported themselves as STJ types when they completed the MBTI (McCaulley, Macdaid, and Kainz 1985). Only 3 percent reported themselves as NFP types. This finding is often repeated when principals of regular schools are typed. It is little wonder the NFP types often believe they are not speaking the language of their principals and department heads. They aren't!

Verne needs to enter a staff meeting debate with cool, calm, and detached analysis. He must start at the beginning, and move step by step to his logical conclusion. Usually, he rushes in and makes intuitive leaps, talking the talk of feeling types:

> I believe. . . .
> It is right that. . . .
> It is my conviction that. . . .
> I just know this will be. . . .

What the feeling person needs to learn is the language of thinking, as shown in Figure 6.1.

When trying to convince his principal, Verne would be wise to talk in terms of supporting data (this means going to the library and finding journal articles that support his point of view). He should quote experts and statistics that show the benefits of an experiential arts program. He has to start thinking of his proposals as essays, with a hypothesis and supporting evidence.

Verne should also consider the dollars and cents. How much will his proposal cost the school? How can costs be cut? How can money be earned? Verne needs to show what he is willing to do to support his idea. For example, he might be willing to work an hour after school, three days a week. The principal has to live within shrinking budgets. Verne has to show an awareness of this if he is to gain the principal's support.

Verne should consider preparing a three-month time line showing how much time he plans to spend on arts and how much time on regular reading programs. If these show signs of improvement in student attitude to learning (e.g., fewer absentees, fewer outbursts, and greater willingness to try to read and write such things as skits, guitar manuals, music lyrics), he will continue with his efforts, increasing time spent on the arts and adding comprehension testing. He will reduce time spent on the arts if there is no sign of student improvement.

Logical consequences and proof of a plan are important for the principal, especially when she answers the calls of concerned parents who wonder how their child, who is already reading poorly, can afford to waste time playing a guitar during language arts class. Verne should give evidence that attention will be given to such

The Feeling Learner ■ **E**xtraversion

■ **I**ntroversion

45 ■ **S**ensing

■ i**N**tuition

■ **T**hinking

■ **F**eeling

■ **J**udging

■ **P**erceiving

FIGURE 6.1

Do's and Don'ts to Convince the Thinking Type

1. Keep things in order. Don't jump ahead in the argument unless you're sure everyone is with you.
2. Be objective. Don't give personal reasons.
3. Stick to the point. Don't ramble.
4. Be frank. Don't skirt issues to protect feelings.
5. Be consistent. Don't try a fresh approach until you've brought closure to the present line of argument.

Red Flag Language

Never begin an important message with these words:
"Regardless of the data. . . ."
"To maintain harmony, I. . . ."
"We must all agree that. . . ."
"Values dictate. . . ."
"My personal view is. . . ."

Instead use:
"The data suggest that. . . ."
"The consequences of this decision are. . . ."
"Several factors to be taken into consideration, including the right or wrong of it, are. . . ."
"Justice will prevail when. . . ."

Golden Rules

■ Be clear
■ Be objective
■ Give consequences

SOURCE: ADAPTED FROM MAMCHUR 1988, P. 52.

details as getting parents' signatures for field trips and assuring that students won't be held up for other classes. The principal needs to feel safe from complaints from other teachers, parents, and possible legal problems. It is Verne's job to make her feel secure.

Although INFPs would agree that all these considerations are important, such details would not be part of their natural methods of persuasion. They believe these details come naturally once the program is approved, so why waste time on them before that? Feeling types believe that conviction is the cornerstone of success. And they have plenty of that. But other types need more. So it's the feeling type's job to provide more.

Feeling types, particularly NFs, resent spending a lot of time on "red tape"—statistics, parental permission forms, and budgets. They would be wise to team up with someone who values and enjoys this part of the process.

Ms. Simpson, an ESFJ who has noticed Verne's growing frustration, wonders if she can be of some help. She is finishing up her master's degree in psychology and her topic, "Using Type Theory to Improve Communication Between Types," might come in handy . . . if only she can find a way to get involved without insulting Verne.

The next time Verne mentions a project, Ms. Simpson gives it a try. "Sounds exciting to me. Would you like some help with that, Mr. Powers?"

Verne smiles. For the first time in months, he really smiles.

RESOURCES

For more information about how different types prefer to work, see *Type Talk at Work* by O. Kroeger and J. Thuesen (New York: Delacorte, 1992).

7

The Judging Learner

▶ **What is judgment in the Jungian sense?**

A preference to deal with the world by decisively acting to create order.

▶ **How does judgment affect behavior?**

The person is inclined to use more energies in controlling than in understanding events.

▶ **How does judging affect the way one interacts, communicates, and teaches?**

It causes the person to want to create an ordered world in which things can happen on time according to a predetermined purpose. Disliking surprises and expecting others to work toward established goals, the judging teacher has clear, well-developed plans for every program. Students will be aware of the goals and will be helped in working toward completion of those goals according to specific procedures within a scheduled time frame that meets the school or district standards.

▶ How does a preference for judgment translate into learning style?

1. Judging students like to plan and schedule and need exact dates regarding course progress, exams, and assignment deadlines. They want to see, in advance, a definite structure, a framework, or an outline of the course of study for each unit—even for the whole year, if possible.

2. Judging students want to complete every task started. They crave a sense of closure. Operating with a strong work ethic, they hate to abandon projects and feel guilty when they do. They dislike casual attitudes toward assignments and will experience more resentment than relief if a teacher assigns something early in the year and then cancels the assignment later on. This is true even if the reason is well justified.

3. Judging students expect a lot of feedback on assignments. They want everything to count and to be evaluated.

▶ How does the teacher respond to these preferences?

The teacher carefully plans the course, giving agendas, timetables, and due dates.

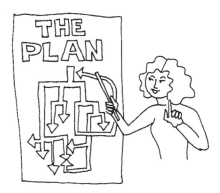

The teacher makes sure he warns the judging students ahead of time regarding where, when, and why things may change. He avoids surprises. He makes everything, including the flexibility, part of the larger plan. Knowing what might happen allows the judging type to relax, feel safe, and go along with the potential changes.

The teacher gives consistent feedback or arranges for peer feedback. If there is a peer feedback process, she gives instructions and guidelines for it beforehand.

Close-up: Judging

Professor Selma Sterne drove carefully down Highway 95. She was planning her strategy as she drove the busy route from

The Judging Learner ■ **E**xtraversion

49 ■ **I**ntroversion

■ **S**ensing

■ i**N**tuition

■ **T**hinking

■ **F**eeling

■ **J**udging

■ **P**erceiving

the university to the school where three of her student teachers were doing their practicums.

Glen Thompson, the school associate, had demanded a meeting. He had just about had it with Michelle Crepeau, the bright but thoroughly unorganized student teacher Selma had assigned to his classroom. In fact, he was sure the student teacher was acting irresponsibly out of some kind of struggle of the wills.

Michelle had left Selma's office moments before her school associate had called. She had come to Selma desperate and nearly reduced to tears. "Mr. Thompson is putting me in a straitjacket," she told Selma. "He's power tripping all the time, focusing on all the wrong things, making me feel inadequate."

Selma had heard such complaints before. It wasn't all that unusual to have the classroom teacher and the student teacher see the same situation from two very different points of view. Selma had a hunch she might know the reason behind some of the misunderstandings. She had used the Myers-Briggs Type Indicator as part of the research she was doing in professional development. The MBTI told her that Glen Thompson was a judging type, Michelle Crepeau a perceiving type. The combination wasn't all that unusual. Judging types are by nature responsible and willing to take on extra work, so in schools they often volunteer or are selected for such professional tasks as supervising student teachers.

Selma's research indicated that the type distribution of school associates was three judging types to one perceiving type. Student teachers, on the other hand, were equally distributed between perception and judgment. It's not surprising that perceiving student teachers were often matched with judging teacher associates.

Later that week, Selma decided to conduct the meeting between Glen and Michelle as a mini-lesson. She used type theory to help both Glen and Michelle stand back from the situation and not take things so personally. Instead of saying such things as "Mr. Thompson likes to have things well scheduled, on track, or on time, " Selma explained the nature of the judging type, his need for structure, for being sure there is a plan with a purpose in place. Judging types value punctuality and sticking to the agenda, and they interpret these behaviors as evidence of responsibility.

Perceiving types, on the other hand, have a very different view of how best to operate. Valuing flexibility, they enjoy living in the moment and have the ability to quickly respond to changing circumstances. Perceiving types feel most responsible when they can alter a plan, respond to immediate needs, and discover the teaching moment.

Talking in objective terms of type differences, rather than subjective terms of personal differences, Selma was able to calm both people that day.

As time went on, Glen and Michelle used their growing knowledge of the judging and perceiving differences to work through their disagreements. The first step was to shed their feelings of engaging in a power struggle. Once they put aside personal feelings, they had a better chance of working together.

In trying to help Michelle with her lesson plans but still give her the freedom she seemed to need, Glen came up with a metaphor that was very useful to Michelle. He compared a lesson to a good story. A good story needs a beginning, a middle, and an end. Students need a sense of structure and a feeling of closure. Within that structure, Michelle, as the writer, could invent and create. She could enjoy the sense of discovery that would feed her sense of achievement. Michelle liked the metaphor. She also appreciated Glen's trying to understand her. They were beginning to work together and form a team.

When judging and perceiving types work together, they must remember two very important points: the judging type needs structure to feel safe; the perceiving type needs spontaneity to feel life is worth living. Trying to make sure both have what they need makes for good working conditions. What's more, if the perceiving type wants the judging type to be more flexible, the path to that flexibility is to have some basic structure in place.

In the classroom, the judging teacher is basically in charge and the perceiving student teacher must make that teacher feel confident that the students will not suffer. The judging type, wanting the perceiving type to do the best possible job, needs to learn to appreciate her ability to be flexible and responsive.

Selma left behind her a copy of a piece called "I'll Do It My Way" for Glen and Michelle to read (Mamchur 1988b). This piece opened the door to many discussions about teaching and the nature of the job. Michelle liked the introduction:

> The dream of every student teacher is to enter a teacher education program, learn the five or ten or fifty essential truths of good teaching, add a personal touch, and zappo—become transformed into one of those founts of knowledge and inspiration—a teacher!
>
> Well, it just isn't so.
>
> Teaching isn't about rules, truths, methods. Teaching is about people working closely with other people.

> Part of the complexity of the practicum lies in the fact that so many people are thrust together in interacting roles. You, the student, are afraid, a bit bewildered, full of hopes and ideals. A class of pupils weaves a force called the group, with its own energy and influence, ready to accept—not to accept—you.
>
> The sponsor teacher, usually experienced, often confident, may or may not be eager to have a student teacher in the classroom.
>
> And finally there is the faculty supervisor from the university often playing the role of expert and evaluator.
>
> This chapter strips us of the roles and looks instead, at us as people. Naked, we act out of a more basic instinct than the roles we each play in the classroom. Regardless of how elaborate the costume, under it lies the skin of the individual (pp. 49–50).

Glen liked the conclusion:

> What an exciting career you have chosen. It is a career filled with the possibility of continuous growth, development, and understanding. It is a career filled with people working with people. Just when you think you've got them figured out–they surprise you one more time. If that frightens you, think carefully about choosing this profession. If that frightens you and fascinates you, it will probably continue to do so for a very long and a very wonderful time (p. 62).

Both agreed they were two of the lucky ones who found teaching both frightening and fascinating.

- **E**xtraversion
- **I**ntroversion
- **S**ensing
- i**N**tuition
- **T**hinking
- **F**eeling
- **J**udging
- **P**erceiving

The principal of the school, upon learning about the work that Selma was doing, was surprised that she made no attempt to "match" types. He suggested the possibility to Selma, who explained that the matching strategy did not guarantee success. Two judging types who have very different purposes or plans based on opposing philosophies can have real difficulties. Two perceiving types, too, can get into trouble. Perceiving types may appear to be without a plan, even when they have one. Most often, perceiving types do have a plan, a secret plan. You'll find out about it if you try to force them to change it. Two perceiving types who are operating from plans they don't want to share—because they want the freedom to deviate from those plans when necessary—can find themselves frustrating one another more than a judging and a perceiving type might.

There are no quick fixes to type theory. Simply matching types does not guarantee agreement. The idea of using type theory is to better understand motive and need, to appreciate and value differences, and to learn from one another.

8

The Perceiving Learner

▶ **What is perception in the Jungian sense?**

A preference to deal with the world by following one's curiosity and seeking understanding."

▶ **How does perception affect behavior?**

The person is inclined to put off decision making until she has had a chance to explore and investigate all the avenues of information. Because the pleasure of process feels much more satisfying than having a final product, the perceiver may start more projects than she finishes. Dropping something that no longer seems interesting is natural for the perceiving type. Curious and adaptive, she enjoys a flexible lifestyle that she finds engaging and pleasurable.

The Perceiving Learner

53

■ **E**xtraversion
■ **I**ntroversion
■ **S**ensing
■ i**N**tuition
■ **T**hinking
■ **F**eeling
■ **J**udging
■ **P**erceiving

▶ How does the perceiving aspect of type affect the way one interacts, communicates, and teaches?

It causes the person to resist structure and to favor changing circumstances in the quest for spontaneity and surprise. Best able to deal with needs as they arise, the perceiving teacher thrives on being able to find the teaching moment in most situations. Resisting too much structure, she designs courses that are flexible, interesting, and adaptive to the various needs of the students. The perceiving teacher feels comfortable with the structure that a regular classroom demands only if that structure is flexible enough to allow the changes she thinks are important.

▶ How does a preference for perception translate into learning style?

1. Driven by a natural curiosity, perceiving students enjoy the process of discovering new ideas, but without a lot of pressure. Perceiving types are good at exploratory learning. They should not be expected to complete everything or to always produce a final product. Testing should be kept to an absolute minimum.

2. Because perceiving students tend to avoid schedules, they may need encouragement in a very structured course. Helping them stay "on task" and "on time" must be done pleasantly, not punitively. Perceiving students need degrees of freedom and appreciate any form of flexibility and spontaneity the teacher can provide.

3. Perceiving students are quite relaxed and open to a variety of styles and ideas. They find pleasure in most situations, provided the structure is not so rigid that they feel all chances for fun and spontaneous adventure have been destroyed. Perceiving students can rarely be bullied into compliance. If bullied or pressured, they will silently withdraw, give up, or cause a rebellion.

▶ How does the teacher respond to these preferences?

The teacher must provide plenty of opportunities for perceiving students to explore and discover. She can offer a variety of possibilities and give students time to dabble in each, play with the ideas, and select one aspect of the unit for more thorough consideration.

The teacher would be wise to establish a real sense of trust and resist the temptation to always be checking up on progress or testing for mastery. Perceiving students respond well to alternatives that allow them to appraise their own work.

If the teacher is a judging type, she must give up the notion of forcing perceiving students to behave like judging students. Instead, she must strive to integrate a real sense of spontaneity and surprise into the classroom.

Close-up: Perceiving

Susan Maddock was dedicated to making her school run well. She'd been principal of Lincoln High for three years now, but she wasn't satisfied with how her staff were relating to each other. Several people just didn't seem to care enough. They said little in meetings and volunteered few ideas. Susan valued dedication and commitment; she expected it from herself and her teachers.

Susan called up the local teacher center and arranged for workshops on team building at her school. Eileen Mallory, the consultant who came to the school, used type theory as a tool. She administered the Myers-Briggs Test Inventory to the entire staff, including the principal and the janitor. The resulting profile told the consultant a lot about the dynamics of the school:

ENFJ   Principal
ENTJ   Vice-principal
ESTJ
ESFJ   Department heads
ISTJ
INFP   English teacher
ISFP   Home economics teacher
ESTP   Physical education teacher
ISTP   Math teacher
ESFJ, ESFJ, ENTJ English, Social
    Studies, and French teachers
ISFJ   Secretary
INTP   Janitor

The Group Profile for the staff looked like this:

The Perceiving Learner

55

■ **E**xtraversion

■ **I**ntroversion

■ **S**ensing

■ i**N**tuition

■ **T**hinking

■ **F**eeling

■ **J**udging

■ **P**erceiving

In this type wheel, a triple bond shows three aspects of type similarity; a double bond, two aspects; a single bond, one aspect; and a dotted line, no similarities. As you can see, the principal has three aspects of type in common with her ENTJ vice-principal and three in common with her ESFJ and ENTJ teachers. These "bonds" give this group the capacity to form a strong united front; they're likely a formidable group should one wish to debate educational policy with them. The two ESFJ teachers and ESFJ department head feel allied with the ENFJ principal and confident they can have their way in this group.

The ISTP math teacher has no common bond with the ENFJ principal. Communication between them may be very difficult unless they learn to correctly interpret and understand their natural differences.

Looking at this type wheel helps the consultant see possible areas of tight groupings and possible areas of feeling isolated or misunderstood. On this staff, the J types overcame their differences when it came to sensation and intuition and thinking and feeling, particularly because there were so many EJ types. The ISTJ managed to "join" the group because of her strong will and J orientation. The IP types felt very isolated. The INFP and ISFP met regularly to console one another and were developing a martyr behavior pattern. The ESTP, so naturally gregarious, felt unpopular and rallied to the ISTP, who also felt like an outcast.

The whole dynamic was becoming unhealthy. Armed with the knowledge of the group profiles and the information offered by the principal, the consultant went to work. She decided to break the participants into four groups: IP, EP, IJ, and EJ. She gave them the task of imagining themselves on a February professional development retreat paid for by the school board; the purpose was to get rejuvenated for the rest of the year. Each group was asked to describe the retreat they would really enjoy attending.

The EJ group presented their ideal retreat, and it looked like this:

EXTRAVERTED JUDGING RETREAT

— *Clear agenda*

— *Planned activities*

— *Attendees list*

— *Compulsory attendance*

— *Feedback*

— *Planned breaks*

— *Variety*

— *Lots to do*

— *Active participation*

— *Discussion opportunity*

— *Planned play activities*

— *Quality planning*

— *Things go well*

The IP group looked like this:

INTRODUCTED PERCEIVING RETREAT

— *Rural setting*

— *Healing/rejuvenation atmosphere*

— *Bird watching*

— *Water*

— *Privacy*

— *Tolerance*

— *Meditation*

— *Nice accomodations and good food*

— *Lots of free time*

— *Solo times and activities*

— *Music*

— *Pets allowed*

— *Fun!!*

— *Coop games*

— *Options*

As the IP group presented their ideal retreat, their principal, Susan Maddock, became agitated and angry. Finally, she could stand it no longer. She leapt to her feet and shouted at the group, "I'm embarrassed by what you're saying. We paid good money for Dr. Mallory to come here to work with us. The least you can do is take the exercise seriously!" She ended her outburst with one disparaging word, "Birdwatching!"

But of course, the IPs were taking the exercise quite seriously. They were being honest: what would most rejuvenate them were activities such as birdwatching, long walks, and quiet time for reflection.

It was a breakthrough moment. The angry accusations resulted in honest exchanges of frustration on both sides.

Eileen Mallory then asked the groups to describe how they thought they were perceived at staff meetings.

The EJs said that people viewed them as:
- aggressive
- domineering
- talking a lot
- feeling themselves superior
- not trusting others to do the job
- needing to control events
- wanting to stick rigidly to their agenda

The IPs, in turn, said that people saw them as:
- quiet
- nonparticipatory
- resenting time spent in meetings
- not being able to think fast
- not having worthwhile ideas

Both groups had thought the worst. Both felt guilty about some of their behavior. The EJs recognized their own aggressiveness, but felt it was necessary to get the job done. The IPs recognized their own passivity, but felt helpless to change the pattern set by the EJ leaders. Although there was some degree of truth in both

The Perceiving Learner   ■ **E**xtraversion

57   ■ **I**ntroversion

■ **S**ensing

■ i**N**tuition

■ **T**hinking

■ **F**eeling

■ **J**udging

■ **P**erceiving

descriptions, they consisted mostly of misconceptions and exaggerations.

The J types learned that P teachers want to participate and do, but need time to rehearse ideas on their own. The P types also need to be invited into the equation. They need to feel a sense of safety and being valued. They need, too, some flexibility to bring up relevant issues that may not have been included on the agenda. Their quiet natures should never be interpreted as indifference.

As Eileen Mallory worked with the groups, the barriers began to crumble. Participants' true motivations were illuminated, and members of both groups looked at their colleagues with new clarity and awareness. With the realizations came tears, laughter, apologies, and the resolu-

tion to not interpret others' behavior from the perspective of their own type.

Because J types dominate the teaching world, it is important for them to encourage the P types, particularly the IP types, to stay in the profession. IPs are the least represented of all types in the classroom. P teachers can best understand P students, and since SP students drop out of school more often than other types, it is essential that someone be there to encourage the SPs to get through a system not really designed for them.

This story is about P teachers, but there are many stories about P students. Later in this book, you'll find a chapter called "Don't Let the Moon Break Your Heart"; it looks at my favorite P, my daughter Mickey, and her struggle to stay in school.

9

Getting Started

There was no question in Jung's mind that educators were the most potent influences on the child's individuation, and were even more potent than the parents. . . . [T]eachers are in a position to recognize disharmonies in a child's personality and to help him strengthen the weaker elements. . . . [T]he most important function of the teacher, however, is to recognize the individuality of each of his pupils and to foster the balanced development of this individuality (Hall and Nordby 1973, p. 87).

Designing a curriculum that meets the needs of all 16 types is usually too daunting a task for most busy teachers when they first begin to use type theory in the classroom. Accommodating different types is a skill that improves with practice. The teacher has many options for where to begin. I have suggested several in the context of the close-ups in this book. The best option, however, is to begin wherever you feel comfortable and wherever your interest lies. Extraversion and introversion are easy starting points. It is also important to focus on sensation and intuition.

In adapting to meet the needs of students, teachers must be careful not to sacrifice their personal strengths and talents in the process. Developing a repertoire of styles is a developmental process. Peter Elbow (1987, p. 207) sums up his own growth as a teacher this way:

For teaching I have mostly one voice, one style. My power is wrapped up in that. If I want power, I've got to use my voice. . . . I can grow or change and start to use other voices or styles slowly. In short, I need to accept

Getting Started

59

■ **E**xtraversion
■ **I**ntroversion
■ **S**ensing
■ i**N**tuition
■ **T**hinking
■ **F**eeling
■ **J**udging
■ **P**erceiving

myself as I am before I can tap my
power or start to grow.

We do best in our own styles. In working from a position of strength, we become
more willing to bend and yield to the needs
of others.

Teachers often ask if they should
encourage students to adapt to a variety of
styles. Isn't this a natural and a more
rigorous training? Won't they need to be
able to cope with all styles in the "real"
world? Do we simply rely on a variety of
teachers to, over time, provide a variety of
models and experiences?

I would like to answer these questions
with a look at important research conducted by Solomon and Kendall (1976). In
their report on individual characteristics
and children's performance in varied
educational settings, they examined remedial, compensatory, and preferential modes
of aptitude-treatment interactions. The
remedial model focused on teaching defi-
cient skills; the compensatory model on
bypassing deficiencies and working in
situations that do not require the defi-
ciency; and the preferential on matching
skills to situations that used strengths and
natural inclinations.

Although the preferential model was
most successful, students often benefited
from a "mismatch" model, where they had
to perform in areas where they were un-
skilled and not naturally inclined. Timing
seemed to be crucial in the mismatch
cognitive model. Early in students' development, a preferential model is best. Likewise,
students do best when learning styles match
preferences at the time students begin to
learn a new body of work. Once students

feel a degree of strength, a compensatory
model can be introduced. The compensatory model calls for students to use methods and skills unnatural to them and is, in
essence, a mismatch of styles.

A mismatch would certainly occur if the
teacher, whose style will surely be different
from that of some of her students, always
teaches according to her own preferred
learning style. Such a practice can be
difficult for students during times of challenging learning, particularly in the early
stages of that process.

I add one more cautionary note to the
"go with your own style" approach: IN types
have a style dramatically different from the
most common type, the ES. Because
extraverts outnumber introverts three to
one, and because sensing types outnumber
intuitives four to one, it is likely that a
majority of students in any normal population classroom will be ES types (Lawrence
1982, p. 40).

INs prefer learning that is abstract,
theoretical, and philosophical. INs learn
well and easily from books, lectures, and
experts—all the "normal" learning activities. Intuitives, particularly introverted
intuitives, usually move to a position of
influence in the school system, creating
curriculum for a largely ES population.
Curriculum developers, professors, researchers, writers, and trainers of teachers
need to recognize the practical, hands-on
preferences of the pragmatic ES type.

McCaulley (1981) expresses a deep
concern for the differences in learning
preference between the shapers of education and the receivers of that education.
Figuratively, those differences might look
like this:

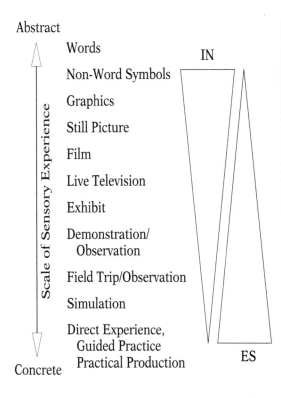

Abstract

Words

Non-Word Symbols

Graphics

Still Picture

Film

Live Television

Exhibit

Demonstration/
Observation

Field Trip/Observation

Simulation

Direct Experience,
Guided Practice
Practical Production

Concrete

Scale of Sensory Experience

IN

ES

SOURCE: Gordon Lawrence and Marie C. Weychart, "On Teaching and Learning," presented at MBTI-IV, the Fourth Bienniel National Conference on the Use of the Myers-Briggs Type Indicator, Association for Psychological Type, Palo Alto, Calif, July 1981.

IN types must also be willing to admit to a possible bias in values. They often view their methods as "superior" to the ES methods. It is easy for them to assume that once they educate ES students in the ways of independent, abstract thinking, the students will "improve and broaden" their methods of learning. Their ES students would, in effect, become more like them.

IN types, particularly INTs, may not want to pay attention to "all this individual differences stuff," wishing instead that students would just dig in and learn in what the INTs describe as "the proper way."

Indeed, the INT methods of learning are traditional and have proven to work well for many people over many years. These traditions have failed some people, however. INTs do not like to fail as teachers—do not like to be incompetent in any way—and thus they can become willing to learn ways to adapt to individual differences, especially when the changes they make lead to success.

When teachers pay attention to individual differences, all sides benefit. Once they are aware of the power and success related to adapting curriculum to meet the needs implied by individual differences, many teachers design courses in which all needs are met some of the time. This is a varied approach consciously designed to let each type have the advantage at different times. It works best when teachers let students in on what they are doing and why. Discussion of learning styles is an important part of this approach.

There is another aspect to the way learning is influenced by type differences. Student learning is affected by the degree to which the student is interested in and attracted to a subject. Type preferences are related to interest in different content areas as well as to the way the content is taught. When considering the importance of match or mismatch, it is useful to remember that certain subjects will turn on some types and turn off others.

For example, S types love practical subjects. History is often the preferred subject of ES students because reading about what real people did in other times captures their interest. The liberal arts are usually attractive to NF and IN types, and business often appeals to ES and ST types (Myers 1985, p. 110).

Because students' success is also deeply

- **E**xtraversion
- **I**ntroversion
- **S**ensing
- i**N**tuition
- **T**hinking
- **F**eeling
- **J**udging
- **P**erceiving

influenced by application (persistence in fixing attention and assiduity in performing what is required), Myers considered application to be an important factor to keep in mind when considering the importance of individual preferences.

Dunn (1983, p. 60), who focuses her research on environmental, emotional, sociological, physical, and psychological learning preferences, has found that most students are capable of analyzing their own learning style:

> In testing more than 175,000 youngsters in grades 3–12, we found that most children not only can tell you how they learn, they want to and are delighted that you asked.
>
> What causes problems is that no one is affected by all the elements of learning style. Obviously students can't tell you about any personal reactions to elements that aren't important to them. But when an element is ei-

ther a very strong preference or a very negative preference, most children can describe their feelings about it and reactions to it very well.

If teachers choose to involve students in identifying their own learning style, they should be sure to share with students what they know about learning style. Sharing gives students the gift of informed choice. Choice is important in education. It is the springboard to thought, the training ground for responsible adulthood. But informed choice is even better. It is the springboard to wise decision making. As Bruno Bettelheim (1960, p. 73) said, "Decision making is a function which, like some nerves or muscles, tends to atrophy when it lies fallow. Or in terms of psychoanalytical theory, decision making is not just an ego function; on the contrary, it is the function that creates the ego and, once created, keeps it going and growing."

References

Bettelheim, B. (1960). *The Informed Heart: Autonomy in a Mass Age.* New York: Avon Books.

Elbow, P. (1986). *Embracing Contraries: Explorations in Learning and Teaching.* New York: Oxford University Press.

Hall, C., and V. Nordby. (1973). *A Primer of Jungian Psychology.* New York: New American Library.

Hunt, D. (1987). *Beginning with Ourselves in Practice, Theory, and Human Affairs.* Cambridge, Mass: Brookline Books.

Jung, C. (1971, originally published 1921). "Psychological Types." In *The Collected Works of C.G. Jung, Vol. 6.* Edited by R.F.C. Hull. Princeton, N.J.: Princeton University Press.

Keirsey, D., and M. Bates. (1978). *Please Understand Me.* Del Mar: Prometheus Nemesis Books.

Kroeger, O., and J. Thuesen. (1992). *Type Talk at Work.* New York: Delacorte Press.

Lawrence, G. (1983). *People Types and Tiger Stripes.* 3rd ed. Gainesville, Fla.: Center for Applications of Psychological Type.

Lawrence, G., and M. C. Weychart. (July 1981). "On Teaching and Learning." Presented at MBTI-IV, the Fourth Biennial National Conference on the Use of the Myers-Briggs Type Indicator, Association for Psychological Type, Palo Alto, Calif.

McCaulley, M. (1974). *Four Preferences Are Scored to Arrive at a Person's Type.* Gainesville: Typology Laboratory, University of Florida.

McCaulley, M. (1977). *The Myers Longitudinal Medical Study, Monograph 11.* Gainesville, Fla.: CAPT.

McCaulley, M. (1981). Presentation at APT Conference, Palo Alto, Calif.

McCaulley, M., G. Macdaid, and R. Kainz. (1985). *Myers-Briggs Type Indicator Atlas.* Gainesville, Fla.: Center for Applications of Psychological Type.

Mamchur, C. (1984). *Insights: Understanding Yourself and Others.* Toronto: Ontario Institute for Studies in Education Press.

Mamchur, C. (May 1988a). "Administrative Mind Reading: How to Talk When the Big Decision Depends On It." *NASSP Bulletin* 72, 508: 52–57.

Mamchur, C. (1988b). "I'll Do It My Way," in *Becoming a Teacher,* edited by P. Holborn, M. Wideen, and I. Andrews. Toronto: Kagan and Woo.

Mamchur, C. (February 1994). "Don't You Dare Say Fart." *Language Arts* 71, 2: 95–101.

Meisgeier, C., and E. Murphy. (1987). *Murphy Meisgeier Type Indicator for Children.* Palo Alto, Calif.: Consulting Psychologists Press.

Myers, I. (1962). *The Myers-Briggs Type Indicator.* Palo Alto, Calif.: Consulting Psychological Press.

Myers, I. (1976). "Relation of Psychological Type to Drop-Out Rate in Nursing." Preliminary Research Report. Gainesville, Fla.: Center for Applications of Psychological Type.

Myers, I. (1980). *Gifts Differing.* Palo Alto, Calif.: Consulting Psychologists Press.

Myers, I. (1985). *Manual, A Guide to the Development and Use of the Myers-Briggs Type Indicator.* Palo Alto, Calif.: Consulting Psychologists Press.

Page, E. C. (1992). *Looking at Type.* 2nd ed. Gainesville, Fla.: Center for Applications of Psychological Type.

Solomon, D. and A. Kendall. (1976). *A Final Report: Individual Characteristics and Children's Performance in Varied Educational Settings.* Rockville, Md.: Spencer Foundation Project.

Zeisset, C. (Fall 1985). "Look at Your Students Through the Four Quadrants." *The Type Reporter* 2, 2: 4.

Part 2

Special Readings

10

A Playground for Teachers

After reading the first part of this book, some of you, especially extraverts and those with some prior knowledge of type theory, may want to start using type theory right away in your classroom. Others may prefer to play around in this chapter for awhile.

I've included this chapter in the book to give teachers the opportunity to become more familiar with type theory before making the leap to classroom use. You can do this by first determining your own type preferences using the Instant Insight Inventory (I.I.I.), a self-scoring mini-instrument designed only for playful use of type theory. For more rigorous assessments, you must complete the full Myers-Briggs Type Indicator, the only truly reliable indicator of type preferences.* Other instruments, like the I.I.I., are reliable only if you score with very high preference—for instance, at least 4 of 5 questions indicating extraversion.

After completing the inventory, you can become more familiar with type theory by playing with it. I've included several exercises that let you experience type theory in situations where the stakes are not as high as they are in the classroom. I've used these exercises in workshops and I can promise that they are a very safe way for you to gain new knowledge.

Some folks get a little nervous committing themselves to exploring psychological differences. *What will I discover?* they wonder. *Will all my secrets be exposed? Will knowing this information change who I am?* Type theory does not judge; it informs. It is not a trait theory; it is a process theory. It explains how one prefers to do things. The exercises are designed and field-tested to

_____

*The MBTI is available from the Center for Applications of Psychological Type, 2815 N.W. 13th St., Suite 401, Gainesville, FL 32609.

help you understand the ways of working and living that work best for you.

This chapter is based on the firm belief that how a teacher perceives and understands herself and others is important. This chapter honors the notion that to be a good teacher, every teacher must take time for herself.

This chapter invites you to discover your own personality preferences, to play with the ideas, to try them out when very little is at stake for you. You might observe your students, have chats with your grand-

mother, take note of your own processes. Examine what motivates you, what drives your educational decisions. Once you feel comfortable with the ideas of type theory as they apply to you, bring those ideas to the classroom.

My experience in working with teachers is that they feel better equipped to develop curriculum using type theory once they understand their own preferences. To that end, I offer the Instant Insight Inventory to help you discover your own type preferences.

A Playground for Teachers

67

- **E**xtraversion
- **I**ntroversion
- **S**ensing
- i**N**tuition
- **T**hinking
- **F**eeling
- **J**udging
- **P**erceiving

Determining Your Own Type Using the Instant Insight Inventory (I.I.I.)

For an estimation of your type preferences, examine the following patterns and choose one or the other. Sometimes you will feel you do both, or that your choice would depend upon the situation. This is to be expected. Remember that typology is a dynamic, changing aspect in your life. Maturation suggests you can move from one function to the other according to need. However, one is preferred, demands less energy, is more natural. Try to answer according to the way you act in an everyday situation. You may have trained yourself to be very organized in your job—but how are you on a holiday, for example? How does it feel BEST to be? Do not deliberate too long over answers. Do not omit any questions. Try to answer according to the way you really are, the way that is wonderful for you. An understanding of your psychological preferences will help you to use the way you are to best advantage. Stage one is recognition.

Introversion and Extraversion

For each set of statements, circle either A or B to indicate which statement is most like you.

1. A. I answer a question quickly, sometimes without thinking.
   B. I like to think about something before I offer an answer or an opinion.

2. A. I use trial and error with confidence.
   B. I like to deeply understand something before I try it.

3. A. I need to find out what others expect of me.
   B. I like to do things on my own.

4. A. I get full of energy when I am around a lot of people, such as at a party.
   B. I get tired when I am around a large group of people, and need to get away often to be by myself and collect my thoughts.

5. A. I enjoy a lot of variety and action.
   B. I enjoy a quiet place all my own where I can reflect uninterrupted.

If you circled A three or more times, your preference is for extraversion.
If you circled B three or more times, your preference is for introversion.

Intuition and Sensation

For each set of statements, circle either A or B to indicate which statement is most like you.

1. A. I enjoy looking at details and seeing proof that things are really as they appear to be.
   B. I tend to skim over details and look for hidden meanings to things.

2. A. I enjoy checking, inspecting, and reading the fine print to find out all the information I can.
   B. I become impatient with routine, repetition, and slow, precise activities.

3. A. I enjoy things as they are, recall past events, and learn from the combination of these two in a "commonsense" sort of way.
   B. In a flash of insight, I go with my "hunches" on many things.

4. A. It would be fairly accurate to describe me as being realistic and practical.
   B. It would be fairly accurate to describe me as being imaginative and inventive.

5. A. I rarely rely on inspiration to keep me going.
   B. I have a lot of bursts of energy, with slack periods in between.

If you circled A three or more times, your preference is for sensation.
If you circled B three or more times, your preference is for intuition.

■ **E**xtraversion
■ **I**ntroversion
■ **S**ensing
■ i**N**tuition
■ **T**hinking
■ **F**eeling
■ **J**udging
■ **P**erceiving

Thinking and Feeling

For each set of statements, circle either A or B to indicate which statement is most like you.

1. A. Much of what I do is ruled by my need for justice.
   B. Harmony is one of the most important aspects of my life.

2. A. I try to logically analyze all the facts in making a decision.
   B. In making a decision, I think of what is best for all the people involved.

3. A. I consider fair and honest criticism to be a natural, acceptable part of human relationships.
   B. I avoid confrontation and feel very uncomfortable giving or receiving criticism.

4. A. I know lots of people who are too soft-hearted and emotional to make good decisions.
   B. I have my feelings hurt by people who tend to analyze or make cold statements when understanding is what I am looking for.

5. A. It's often difficult for me to freely express my emotions.
   B. I find it easy to express my feelings and to understand others' feelings.

If you circled A three or more times, you prefer the thinking approach to decision making. If you circled B three or more times, your preference is for the feeling approach.

Perceiving and Judging

For each set of statements, circle either A or B to indicate which statement is most like you.

1. A. I like to be in control of the events in my life and make them "the way they ought to be."
   B. I need to understand thoroughly the events in my life and therefore spend more time than I should making decisions.

2. A. Once I make up my mind, I find it difficult to change it.
   B. I put off decision making as long as possible and change my mind often.

3. A. I like schedules and some definite order or system to regulate the way I do things.
   B. I prefer to live by an easygoing, flexible pattern.

4. A. I choose work to come before play when I organize my time and priorities.
   B. Meeting deadlines are mad-rush affairs for me because of my "there's plenty of time" attitude.

5. A. I most enjoy friends who share my ideals and standards and are true to them.
   B. I choose friends who have interests similar to mine and with whom I can share common experiences.

If you circled A three or more times, your preference is for the judging pattern.
If you circled B three or more times, you prefer the perceiving pattern.

Now that you have determined your orientations (Extraverted or Introverted), your functions (Sensing or iNtuition; Thinking or Feeling), and your interface (Judging or Perceiving), your overall type will begin to emerge in a kind of skeletal form—ENTP, ISFP, and so on. For a brief account of your type's overall characteristics, look up your "initials" and read the description under the corresponding letters on the chart that follows.

If you are a bit uncertain as to which is your preferred type, look now at your least preferred or opposite type. Your opposite should definitely not be you. If, for example, you think you are an ENFP, your total opposite will be ISTJ. The ISTJ is found to the left of the ENFP descriptor, E is always opposite I, S is opposite N, T is opposite F, and J is opposite P. The "opposite" of you in this context is sometimes called your shadow type. This shadow would describe the way in which you find it difficult and energy-consuming to function. If you think you might, for example, be an INFP/ENFP borderline, go to the ISTJ and the ESTJ and see which you find most foreign. Your "opposite" type description should feel the least like you.

■ **E**xtraversion
■ **I**ntroversion
■ **S**ensing
■ i**N**tuition
■ **T**hinking
■ **F**eeling
■ **J**udging
■ **P**erceiving

Brief Descriptions of the Sixteen Types As They Apply to Teaching Styles

ENTJ

Intellectual CHALLENGER, insists upon critical thinking and concept development. A divergent thinker and ORGANIZER who wants a systematic, analytical plan of action at all times.

ESTJ

Realistic, INFORMATION GIVER, wants a regulated, logical system that is fair and disciplined. A determined MANAGER, wants a practical, purposeful, well-run classroom.

INTP

Inquiring THEORETICIAN, emphasizes discovery and independence. Analytic, reflective, curious SCIENTIST, wants an open-ended, comprehensive, discovery-oriented classroom.

ISTP

Practical TRAINER, values exactness and economy. Objective, nonjudgmental ANALYZER, runs a fair and straightforward classroom.

ISFP

Nurturing SUPPORTER, values practical learning in a positive environment. Observant, realistic, gentle COOPERATOR, creates a useful and caring educational setting.

INFP

Imaginative FACILITATOR, emphasizes creative thinking and moral development. Original and nondirective INVENTOR, creates a reflective and harmonious educational environment.

ESFJ

Empathetic MANAGER, values cooperative and supportive communications. Practical and well organized, a conscientious HARMONIZER, wants a personal, collaborative environment.

ENFJ

Caring STIMULATOR, values self-expression and imagination. Analytical, inventive, expressive HARMONIZER, runs a disciplined, original classroom.

ESTP

Realistic INFORMATION giver, good-natured, tolerant, practical, values firsthand experience. Competitive OBSERVER, stresses skill acquisition and purposeful work.

ESFP

Adaptive SUPPORTER, stresses self-development and positive interactions. Friendly and easygoing REALIST, enjoys practical, hands-on learning situations.

ISTJ

Analytical MANAGER, stresses punctuality, fairness, and practicality. Organized and competitive REALIST, concerned with running a stable, conservative classroom.

ISFJ

Conscientious and supportive MANAGER, values positive interaction and collaboration. Conservative NURTURER, runs a stable, practical, purposeful classroom.

INFJ

Stimulating INFLUENCER, expressive, values-driven, stresses clarity and moral development. Serious and quietly forceful INNOVATOR, creates a well ordered, respectful, and stimulating class environment.

INTJ

Critical CHALLENGER, driven by a need for logic and love of knowledge. Determined INQUIRER, concerned with the way the organization serves the individual, runs a thoughtful classroom.

ENFP

Enthusiastic FACILITATOR, enjoys orchestrating educational change. Impulsive ENERGIZER, stimulates and encourages personal growth, development, and creative thinking.

ENTP

Competitive CHANGE AGENT, enjoys intellectual challenges. Inventive ANALYZER, strives to understand and inspire students and colleagues.

A Playground for Teachers

73

■ **E**xtraversion
■ **I**ntroversion
■ **S**ensing
■ i**N**tuition
■ **T**hinking
■ **F**eeling
■ **J**udging
■ **P**erceiving

Playing with Type

Now that you have determined your type preferences, have fun with them. Explore differences in playful ways. See for yourself how they work.

Extraversion and Introversion Activity

You might try this activity at a family picnic. The larger the group, the better this exercise works. Have everyone answer the questions in the first part of the Instant Insight Inventory to identify whether they are more extraverted or introverted. Then have all the introverts gather together to discuss how they feel when they are around a lot of extraverts. Ask the introverts to describe how they feel when they're with a lot of extraverts. Have each group report back to the whole group.

Because this exercise is both a great ice breaker and a quick way to show groups the power and reality of type differences, I have used it many times to introduce type theory to groups of teachers, parents, and superintendents. The responses I receive are remarkably similar.

Hundreds of introverts commonly use the following words to describe how they feel around a lot of extraverts: entertained, threatened, overwhelmed, judged, restless, and smug. The introverts often say they feel put on the spot, inferior, inadequate, rushed, and pressured because they are expected to "perform" with no time to prepare. Ironically, they also report feeling smug and superior when extraverts rush into things or talk too much, too fast, or too

foolishly. The introverts can sit back, watching, waiting, not getting involved until the time and opportunity are just right.

Extraverts, too, commonly use these words to describe their feelings: responsible, frustrated, vulnerable, too loud, pushy, on the spot, judged, and superior. The extraverts' feelings are not very different from the introverts' feelings. It's the reasons for the feelings that are different. The introvert feels put on the spot because he needs time to think, but the extravert, in his enthusiasm, doesn't give him time. The extravert feels put on the spot because the introvert *doesn't* speak, so the extravert feels compelled to fill the void, to start the project, to push the issue. This need to act or to speak often fills the extravert with guilt. Occasionally it makes the extravert feel superior. Almost always the introvert's silences make the extravert feel frustrated. Too often, silence makes extraverts feel vulnerable, naked.

I'm an extravert who shouts stories from the kitchen to entertain introverted guests as I stir-fry the chop suey. I jump naked into the Jacuzzi before I realize others are scrambling for their bathing suits. I tell "secrets" because it never occurs to me that they are secrets. I can relate to the words *vulnerable, on the spot, frustrated.* Any extraverts out there relating?

This section is designed to help us play with type in the laughter of recognition. One of the benefits of knowing type is self-understanding, recognition, respect, acceptance. Isn't it good to know there are others out there like you?

Feel free to report by drawing your feelings. Here is how one group of extraverts illustrated their feelings:

And here is a drawing from a group of introverts:

This picture summarizes the feeling of both groups:

Sensing and Intuition Activity

You may want to play around with sensation and intuition. These perceiving functions govern our preferences for giving information. Ask directions of several sensing types. Choose a location unknown to you. Now ask intuitive types to perform the same task. Enjoy the differences.

Sensing types are usually very precise and accurate in giving direction. They will say such things as "pull out of your driveway, turn left, and drive for three blocks until you hit Fourth Avenue. Proceed north. . . ."

As an intuitive, I can barely follow such instructions even when I already know how to get to my destination. I need what I think of as "big" instructions: Point me in the right direction first—a big landmark I know, such as Seattle or the mountains. Then tell me how long it will take to get there—"about 20 minutes in evening traffic." Miles mean nothing to me unless someone in the car sets my mileage meter and I don't get lost—but they usually don't and I usually do.

A Playground for Teachers

75

■ **E**xtraversion
■ **I**ntroversion
■ **S**ensing
■ i**N**tuition
■ **T**hinking
■ **F**eeling
■ **J**udging
■ **P**erceiving

I also need to know when I have missed my destination by going too far. "If you hit Portland, you have missed Seattle. If you get to Richmond Centre, you have missed the airport." That is the kind of direction an intuitive likes to receive.

After having been hopelessly lost on numerous occasions, I've learned to guide the sensing type in giving me direction. By doing this, I usually end up with great instructions and can almost always find my destination on time, a real feat for the highly intuitive type. (Another sure-fire method is to hire a taxi and follow it in your car.)

Sensing and intuitive types often miscommunicate when making arrangements. The essential difference is in attention to detail. Pay attention to how you and members of your family give instructions for getting together.

Here are two classic examples that happen in my family from time to time. They happen less than they used to because we are pretty much aware of the traps our type differences can get us into, but when we are tired or stressed or rushed, our type differences play their nasty games.

I recently agreed to do some consulting for another firm that needed to add a day-long type theory workshop to a three-day retreat. The consultant, an intuitive type, told me that the work would be done in San Francisco. He was making all the arrangements, would pick me up at the airport.

Great. I happily agreed and arranged to take my daughter with me. We would make a holiday of it. She'd shop during the day while I was working. We'd go to the theater in the evening. So far, so good. We arrived. He picked us up and drove us to Santa

Clara. No shops. No theater. No nothing. A big hotel and convention center two hours outside of San Francisco.

To an intuitive, Santa Clara is "sort of" San Francisco. To my sensing daughter, imagining herself stuck in a big hotel for her four-day holiday, "sort of" just wasn't good enough. She couldn't believe I hadn't asked for more specific information. "You know intuitives always lie," she moaned. And so it seems to the literate sensing type. We rented a car and moved to a San Francisco hotel.

Even on the home front, we aren't safe. My daughter and I often divide chores. She does all the shopping while I run off to downtown meetings. Habitually, we'll meet at the end of the day at a coffee shop inside the shopping center in case either of us is a bit behind schedule. Secretly, too, I meet her there so she won't have to stand, waiting. Because my daughter has a form of heart disease that causes her blood pressure to triple when she stands for too long, I try to prevent her getting into tiresome situations. Yet I never admit that reason out loud.

One day, an awful rainy day in November, I was late, rushing for an important and totally unpleasant meeting. I dropped her off on the street outside the shopping center. "Where will we meet?" she called as she left the car. "Here," I yelled, pulling into the traffic, late, anxious, not quite ready for the dreadful meeting. Four o'clock. I rushed to the coffee shop. She wasn't there. I waited. An hour. She's never late. I began to worry, imagining serial killers and collapsing buildings. And then I thought, carefully.

"Here," I'd said. Here. In the street. In the rain. Outside the shopping center. Here. And sure enough, there she was. Wet, cold, waiting. And I wanted to weep for the generalizations my mind makes. For the "here" that meant to me, "Here, the usual spot." And to her that meant "Here, where you left me. Where you can easily pick me up without parking the car. Convenient to you. Here. Literally. Here."

You may collect your own stories about type differences. Please be gentle on yourself if some make you shake your head and wonder, *How could I have done that?* When we are stressed, our "opposite" function often messes us up. If you are an intuitive type, sensation will be your opposite and inferior function. And sometimes, just sometimes, it leaves your daughter standing in the rain.

Thinking and Feeling Activity

Thinking and feeling differences will become apparent as you use your judgment to make decisions and take actions. You will be especially aware of type differences if you have messed up in some big way and are confiding your errors to your "opposite" type. For this activity, try telling your tale of woe to somebody who is your opposite type.

A thinker may listen carefully and then give you his best gift: a critical analysis that usually includes a solution to your problem, a series of steps to ward future error, a personal plan of action to mend your ways.

When the feeling type, who really wants simply to be understood, gets this objective analysis, she often feels a deep sense of resentment and inadequacy. She feels alone.

As a young feeling type married to a young thinking type, I experienced this dreaded sense of loneliness in troubled times more often than most marriages can stand. It took me years to learn to help my hus-band respond to me in ways I could handle. Had you spoken to my frustrated husband during those years of struggling through differences we didn't understand, he might have described my decision-making ability during times of stress as being muddled, sloppy, emotional, unfair, demanding. He constantly hoped I would "grow up" to the state of objective maturity where I could welcome constructive criticism as a healthy way to approach problem solving.

Thinking and feeling differences can feel painful and upsetting to both types in time of real stress. Because I am suggesting that you play with type at this stage, it might be a good idea to explore past mistakes that are no longer very important to you. You might even suggest a game of make-believe if sharing real experiences seems too stressful.

Even when we invent situations in which we've goofed, we feel sensitive about how others respond to our mistakes. When you explore how you respond to the mistakes of others, and they respond to you, it is important to be honest, caring, and patient.

I will never forget my first year of teaching. I was 19 years old, eager, vulnerable, with long legs and a very ample bosom. Now, most 19-year-olds would have felt blessed with such physical attributes. But I wasn't most teenagers. I was the only female teacher in the school except for the home economics and gym teachers, and I was teaching English literature to a group of students who couldn't read—and most of them were older than I was. Moreover, my principal, who had inherited moral standards from his Presbyterian minister father, had warned me that if any student made sexual advances toward me, I would be fired immediately.

A Playground for Teachers

77

■ **E**xtraversion
■ **I**ntroversion
■ **S**ensing
■ i**N**tuition
■ **T**hinking
■ **F**eeling
■ **J**udging
■ **P**erceiving

I slouched when I walked, bowing my shoulders to the point where I looked like a hunchback. Life proceeded without turmoil for a few weeks, but soon my troubles began. Determined to get the better of the teachers, the students discovered my greatest fear: sexual innuendos. They began to torment me. I experienced my worst times during Large Group Detention, a dreaded invention of that period of educational history where up to 50 "delinquent" students were forced to sit useless for an hour after school as punishment. It was my duty to keep the students silent and to take down all their names. Because I didn't know most of the students, I'd pass around a paper for them to sign. The signed sheet would be returned with phone numbers and sweetheart signs, little hearts with arrows through them.

My paranoia grew. One day during Literature 10, Victor, a huge 18-year-old, stood and drawled in a gruff voice, "Uh, Mrs. Mamchur, if I was a carpenter, and you were a lady . . . "

I froze as I heard the faint buzz of the intercom, a clear indication my principal was listening in, a habit he enjoyed.

I looked at Victor, who was coarse-looking and not very bright, and out of my mouth flew these words: "If you're stupid you don't say those words to a lady, but if you're stupid and ugly you don't even think them."

Silence. Stunned silence.

I rushed from the classroom into the washroom. I cried into the sink. I sobbed. I howled. I made a decision.

I marched into the principal's office. "Mr. Friesen, I quit." My face puckered into a howl. "And I have boobs," I screamed. I ran out of his office, out of the school, all the way home, leaving my car in the parking lot.

That night, I confessed to my husband the awful thing that I had done. He responded in true "thinking" fashion. I never said a word. I just listened. This is how the one-sided conversation went:

He: "Well, first let's go get your car."
Me: "My car?" I had forgotten about my car.
He: "I can't imagine you saying a stupid thing like that!"
Me: "Which stupid thing?" Was he talking about what I said to Victor or to Mr. Friesen?
He: "I think we can solve this. Maybe if you type a letter to Mr. Friesen he will be able to understand the situation. Give him a chance to think about it."
Me: "A *solution?*" I don't want a solution. I want to die.
He: "What were you thinking anyway?"

I ran out of our house, the tears once again in high gear. I ran to my mother's house. Again, the whole awful story. Her "feeling" response: "You must have been awfully scared to say something like that."

"Yes! Oh, yes!"

My mother offered no solution, she simply understood. She held me until I was sobbed out. She listened as I phoned Victor and tried to apologize. Victor never forgave me and I guess I couldn't expect him to. When I returned home, Mr. Friesen and my husband were calmly discussing the solution. I went back to work, the threat of being fired withdrawn, and I tried to establish a real relationship with my students.

It is my worst teaching memory, my cruelest, most unthinkable act. An act I couldn't stand. My guilt and self-disgust were, still are, huge.

At such a time, a thinker's critical analysis and problem solving are almost unbearable. What a feeling type needs when he is in such distress is simple understanding.

"You must have been scared." Indeed.

Judging and Perceiving Activity

Judging and Perceiving are those differences that most affect the way we organize our world. The J type needs organization, structure, and closure to feel safe. The P type needs spontaneous adventure to feel that life is worth living. Here, more than in any other aspect of type differences, the value of one is the nonvalue of the other.

Judging and perceiving differences can be a lot of fun. Plan a "judging" day, a "judging" party, a short "judging" holiday.

Plan everything. Write up an agenda. Stick to schedules. Make reservations. Make sure everything has a purpose. Bring closure to all events. Don't start anything you can't finish.

How does it feel? Safe? Did you accomplish a lot? What did you miss?

Now plan a "perceiving" day, a "perceiving" party, a short "perceiving" holiday.

Go with the flow. Discover as you go. Abandon things that cease to interest you. Start several projects, exploring, with no real need to complete or master. Give in to your curiosity. Trust your instincts. Spend time playfully. Keep a journal recording how you feel. Excited? Worried? Did you relax? Were you energized? Share these experiences and observations with other Judging and Perceiving types.

Remember, for the Perceiving type all decisions are tentative and subject to revision if and when new insights and information arise, whereas the Judging type wants adherence to the rules and regulations to ensure a structured, efficient, and well-run activity (or classroom).

Experiencing the opposite way of organizing your work can be very informative. It can also help explain why it can be difficult to travel with friends. For years I surrounded myself, by choice and by birth, with judging types. Then, at age 35, I had a mid-life crisis. I decided to experience a perceiving lifestyle. I bought a small house in the suburbs and shared it with a potter who was an ENFP—just like me!

We never balanced a checkbook. We ate lobster on the first of the month and pork and beans at the end of the month. We decided to renovate. The small rooms bothered us. We wanted open spaces, curved walls, grass cloth, fig trees. We went wild tearing down walls, buying plants, putting up the grass cloth, plastering the curved surfaces. It was beautiful! Open. Free. Faulty. Flawed. Cracking.

We had torn down all the bearing walls!

A strange thing happened to me that year of the cracking ceiling and the resurrected walls. I became a Judging type. I became the balancer of books, the checker of plans. Experiencing or being with your opposite can often free you up to be yourself.

"Gifts differing" is how Isabel Myers described type differences. It's a nice way to look at things. Why not try it?

Cooking with Type

You may want to play with type by examining how you do things—which parts of your preferences influence your actions. Bonnie L. Marsh has put together the following example of type differences in the preparation of pumpkin soup.* Try your own analysis. Enjoy!

---

*Reprinted with permission from Bonnie L. Marsh, *Pumpkin Soup* (Gainesville, Fla.: Center for Applications of Psychological Type, 1984).

■ **E**xtraversion
■ **I**ntroversion
■ **S**ensing
■ i**N**tuition
■ **T**hinking
■ **F**eeling
■ **J**udging
■ **P**erceiving

Pumpkin Soup
ingredients (as printed in an actual book)

1/2 lb. mushrooms, sliced	1 T curry powder	1 c. evap. milk
1/2 c. chopped onions	1 lb. cooked, sieved pumpkin	dash nutmeg
1 T butter	3 c. broth, vegetable or chicken	salt and pepper
1 T flour	1 T honey	

SENSING DIRECTIONS

1. Lay out necessary equipment: heavy pan, knife, caliper, thermometer, carpenter's level, tablespoons, measuring cups.
2. Check ingredients. Consult cookbook or call friend to find out how much nutmeg is in a dash, and how much salt and pepper should go in a batch of pumpkin soup.
3. Chop mushrooms and onions. (Calipers will be helpful here. 3/16 thickness recommended.) Sauté mushrooms and onions in butter. After the sautéing in butter, add one tablespoon flour. This thickens the sauce a bit preparatory to adding the liquids, and results in a thicker soup. You will know the mushrooms are cooked when a table knife encounters resistance when you try to cut one. You will know the onions are done when a table knife passes easily through.
4. Add flour. Add broth. (Be sure the measuring cup is on a level surface when you measure. Carpenter's level will be helpful here.) Add everything else except milk. Add milk and heat without boiling. (Thermometer will be helpful here. Do not let temperature rise above 200 degrees F.)
5. Serve in tureen and bowls pleasing to the eye, and garnish with chopped fresh parsley.

INTUITIVE DIRECTIONS

There is a lot of possibility for creativity in this soup. A good, rich pumpkin soup offers potential for synchronous cooking. Open your refrigerator. Let your imagination roam. Water chestnuts, olives, a dab of mustard, some pieces of chicken. Whatever. If you are going to call this pumpkin soup, it might be helpful to have some pumpkins, but mashed carrots, squash or even sweet potatoes will do. You might want to start by sautéing any ingredient that needs this process. In this way you will need to use only one pan. Add the rest of the ingredients and taste until it seems right to you.

While the soup heats (it is better not to boil it if you've included milk) you will probably want to make some rolls to go with the soup, and while you're in the mood for cleaning the refrigerator, and have to be in the kitchen anyway, you might want to defrost the freezer. In fact, you could probably get a little start on next week's cooking by frying up that frozen hamburger in the freezer. But the frying pan's dirty. But that's OK because you'll be in the kitchen anyway so you can wash the dishes.

And while you're washing dishes, and thinking about the delicious soup on the stove, you can make plans either for a great soup tasting event, or for the restaurant you're going to open. Serve the soup in whatever is clean, or send someone to the store for paper bowls.

THINKING DIRECTIONS

1. Analyze the process. This recipe can be cooked quite efficiently if some thought is given to process. For instance: melt the butter in the pan over low heat while you chop the onions and mushrooms. If the broth has been refrigerated, it will cook more quickly if you let it warm to room temperature.

2. Analyze the equipment. Try to use as few utensils, pans and bowls as possible. For instance, if you first measure the curry powder, then the butter, then the honey with the tablespoon, you will have to wash it only once. (The honey should slide off the butter.)

3. Analyze the recipe. Alterations should be made from the beginning. How many people are you serving? How much will each eat? Is the recipe large enough? Too large?

4. Proceed as with sensing directions.

5. It would be logical to serve this soup from a pitcher.

FEELING DIRECTIONS

You may need to substitute some ingredients according to who will be eating the soup, so these are just guidelines. If there is someone who doesn't like mushrooms, you can leave out the mushrooms, or substitute potatoes. If onions are hard on someone's stomach, you can leave them out or reduce the amount or substitute beau monde seasoning. In fact, you may want to wait until almost the last minute to decide whether or not to serve pumpkin soup. You may want to omit it entirely from your menu and serve another soup, or a dish that seems appropriate at that time. Just right. Serve with a warm smile.

11

Temperaments and Teaching

Greek myth teaches that the gods were sent by Zeus to make humans more like the gods themselves. Each god gave according to his or her own strength. Apollo gave us a sense of spirit. Prometheus taught us truth and science. Epimetheus gave us a sense of duty. And Dionysus, god of wine and song, gave us joy. Each god had a different temperament and each had a different following. Those who followed Dionysus did not enjoy the practices of those who followed the duty-bound Epimetheus.

And so were born the four temperaments of man.

Today, motivational theorists use what they call temperament decoding to organize Jungian type theory with a focus on motivational patterns (Keirsey and Bates 1984, p. 27). Many of these theorists continue to use the godly names of temperament to define the different types because the notions of being driven by spirit or science or duty or joy are true to temperament theory today. These old classifications hold a surprising amount of truth when applied to motivational theory.

I use the terms Traditionalist (SJ), Idealistic Change Agent (NF), Promethean Achiever (NT), and Dionysian Free Spirit (SP) to suggest the essence of each temperament.

The Traditionalist (SJ)

When you combine the practical, realistic, fairly cautious aspect of S (sensation) with the determined, closure-seeking aspect of J (judgment), you have a traditionalist, an SJ temperament. The SJ is driven, above all, by her need to do her duty.

The most common type in education, the SJ comprises 38 percent of the general population and 56 percent of the teaching population (Keirsey and Bates 1978, pp. 39 and 166). All ISFJ, ESFJ, ISTJ, and ESTJ types are SJ traditionalists. Principals tend particularly to be SJ types. Dedicated and committed, they have the longest stay in education, tending not to abandon anything, including their profession.

It is not surprising that the SJ so often becomes the principal, the leader of the school. The SJ is driven to be in charge, to be useful to the society she belongs to. The SJ strives to be in charge because she feels most confident about her own ability to do the job right. It is very difficult for the SJ to delegate, let go, turn any of the responsibility over to others. Unless SJ principals learn to enlist the help of others, they will eventually succumb to the stress of overwork by becoming ill (rashes, ulcer, even a heart attack). Too responsible to allow stress to stop them from working, they continue until they drop. Such expressions as "You are making me sick," "I am worried to death," and "Don't give me an ulcer" are typical SJ responses to stress.

The SJ is tenacious and will insist on continuing with the task at hand because he has assigned himself to doing it. This tenacity has its bright side in that the SJ will persevere when others have given up. This is wonderful when the task is worth all the effort. It's dreadful when the task should have been abandoned ages and dollars ago, or if it was not really a worthwhile task in the first place.

The dark side of the SJ is that he does not know when to give up. The SJ principal is wise to team with a vice-principal who is unlike him (an SP, NF, or NT) who can provide balance and convince the SJ to give up when giving up is what is called for.

The SJ is a belonger, a traditionalist, a conservator. He wants to belong to the society in which he works and lives and he wants to earn the right to belong. The SJ

SJ

Stabilizers, Traditionalists, Consolidators, Organizers, Caregivers

are bound to do their duty.

EXIT

enjoys a practical, bureaucratic, well-defined hierarchy with a central leader. Often, he is that leader. But whoever the leader is, that position must be earned and obeyed.

As a teacher or principal, the SJ temperament organizes interactions around tasks, preferring that one person be in charge of the task and that specific and fixed rules govern the way things are done. She wants the principal to be in charge of the school, the teacher to be in charge of the classroom.

■ **E**xtraversion
■ **I**ntroversion
■ **S**ensing
■ i**N**tuition
■ **T**hinking
■ **F**eeling
■ **J**udging
■ **P**erceiving

Productivity is the organizational goal: producing good citizens who can function with responsibility in the work-a-day world. Growth of responsibility and utility sums up the SJ's educational goal. Having the students get on with the work and learn the basics is a common classroom goal.

Preferring formal structures in the classroom, the SJ principal, teacher, and student enjoy a learning environment that combines structure, predictability, clear-cut assignments, and fairness.

One of the chief jobs the SJ has given himself is to be the stabilizer of his social and educational world. Change, revolution, chaos, and anarchy are the enemies of the SJ traditionalist. He is often very uncomfortable with the new trends in education. The traditionalist temperament balances the lust for change that drives some of the other temperaments. He can be counted on in the educational system to preserve those things that need preserving; he may need some help, however, in deciding what those things are because he will naturally want to keep them all. Ironically, the struggle to keep things as they are is part of this process of selection. The SJ does not win all the battles.

There can be times when the SJ is the greatest advocate of change. When she absolutely believes a change is needed, she will work with remarkable determination to make that change, to create a new system. But once that system is in place, pity the person who tries to get her to change it again.

The slogan of SJs on the job is "We deal with it" and indeed, they do. The SJs in the school can be counted on to deal with whatever must be dealt with. They should be recognized for that and honored. A hard worker, the SJ principal, teacher, parent, or student rarely asks for praise, but can deeply resent being taken for granted.

One of the benefits of knowing temperament theory is that it helps us to understand and accept differences. It also helps us to meet the needs of others. The SJ needs to do the job and be recognized for doing it. The worst thing you can say to an SJ is that she is irresponsible. The best thing you can do is to create a working space in which she can do her job and be valued for doing it well.

It might be fun to seek out a few SJ types and recognize their good work. It might be fun to see the smiles that result. Like everything in life, praise is related to type. Praising according to temperament just makes good teaming sense.

The Idealistic Change Agent (NF)

When you combine the inventive, push-the-envelope attitude associated with intuition, and the high-spirited, values-driven orientation of feeling, you have an idealistic change agent, the NF temperament.

The NF is driven, above all, by his almost indefinable need to grow in a way true to himself. Part of that growth includes the process of finding the self. In a nutshell, the NF pursues the goal of *becoming*.

All INFJ, ENFJ, INFP, and ENFP types are Idealistic Change Agents. Named after Apollo, this Apollonian temperament makes up about 12 percent of the population and 32 percent of teachers (Keirsey and Bates 1978, pp. 60, 166).

Despite their love of change, NF teachers have a relatively long stay in education. They prevent burn-out by changing jobs within the system and, of course, changing the system itself. Dedicated to the humanities, NFs can find their life's calling within their profession and are usually very dedicated to it.

NF

Energizers, Catalysts, Artists, Organizers, Caregivers

are driven to be true to self.

The NF temperament is complex and difficult to understand. Whereas the other three temperament types can understand (though perhaps not approve of) one another, none really understands the NF's craving for constant change in the pursuit of finally discovering the real, true self. Only NFs themselves know the commitment to a goal in constant flux.

Finding their prototype in Apollo, NFs walk the earth full of passion, seeking intense relationships in the process of becoming their true, ideal selves. If they can help the rest of the world find themselves, then all is well. Ironically, for NFs the path to self-identity is often in helping others discover their own truths. NFs hunger to help, but in the larger more spiritual sense, rather than the specific duty-oriented sense experienced by SJs.

Often attracted to one another, the SJ and NF can drive each other mad by their differing attitudes to change. The SJ, often the principal, is seeking constancy, a solid path he can follow. The NF, often the department head of English, Drama, Theater, Music, or Theology, is seeking metamorphosis, the endless pursuit of becoming. The SJ watches in amazement as the NF pursues a live goal with passion and one-minded determination only to abandon it to a new dream when the NF feels any sense of that goal not quite being true to her self. Any hint of falseness, of lacking the deepest personal integrity, is the demon enemy of the NF, who longs for inner harmony and satisfaction.

The NF's goal is to be real. The path to being real is to act, to do, to achieve in ways that bring the NF closer to her real self. As one acts, does, and achieves, however, there is danger of stagnation: the NF can become permanently stuck in that one place. This is a terrible problem for the NF because any one place is not *the* place; it is only a step closer to the true place of self-actualization.

If the NF gets stuck, a terrible feeling of losing oneself in the mundane aspects of living comes over her. This can lead her to abandon job, family, or country. Abandonment or lack of activity, of course, is deeply unsatisfactory to the NF, who feels the awful guilt and stigma that result from such actions. Yet she faces them to overcome her own inner sense of wasting her life in inaction and nonbeing.

■ **E**xtraversion

■ **I**ntroversion

■ **S**ensing

■ i**N**tuition

■ **T**hinking

■ **F**eeling

■ **J**udging

■ **P**erceiving

This paradox is one that haunts the NF. If the NF cannot find a sense of balance, she is in serious trouble. Luckily, the world of learning and education often provides that balance. and that is one reason NFs are so attracted to education and stay in it for so long.

Leaders of causes, NFs use their intuitive skills to invent and predict and design; and their feeling skills to persuade and inspire. The energy source and persuasive element in many school reforms are NF types.

Consistent with their personal goal, their educational goal is for growth of identity and integrity. Almost the opposite of their SJ colleagues, the NFs crave a completely decentralized structure, with no central leader. They are excellent at encouraging the leadership qualities in everyone. They want an organization that is ethical and humanitarian.

Personal and sensitive, they do not function well in critical, competitive situations and rarely allow such climates to exist in their classrooms. They long to be recognized for their creativity, their ability to inspire. Unlike the SJs, who want praise to focus on the goal of doing a job well, NFs want praise to focus on the goal of working with integrity and insight.

What NFs most resent is the accusation that they are dishonest phonies. That accusation will cause irreparable damage between the accuser and the NF. Stress for NFs usually centers around the NFs' conflicts over beliefs or values. NFs sometimes respond to severe stress with paranoid imaginings, or by developing eating disorders or various forms of personality dysfunction. Naturally imaginative, NFs imagine in times of stress as well as in good times.

The way to keep NFs functioning at their most inventive, energetic best is to give them plenty of opportunity to discover, to explore, to use their visionary powers and skills in creating change that is good for their pupils, their classroom, their school, their world.

The Promethean Achiever (NT)

When you combine the inventive, curious nature of intuition and the analytical, determined logic of thinking, you have the Promethean Achiever (NT). The NT is driven, above all, by her drive for power, especially gained through knowledge. This drive for power should not be confused with a need to control, although it can often feel like that. The NT, the most driven of the temperaments, has such a need to achieve, to accomplish, to understand and thereby be in control of life around her, that her tenacity can feel intimidating.

All INTP, ENTP, INTJ, and ENTJ types are Promethean Achievers. Named after Prometheus, the god who brought fire to man, NTs makes up about 12 percent of the population and 8 percent of the teaching population (Keirsey and Bates 1978, pp. 47, 166). The thirst for knowledge often leads NTs to education, but they typically stay only a few years because they are attracted to higher levels of authority and decision making. They often become the inventors of curriculum, the superintendents of schools, the presidents of consulting companies. When they do stay in education, it is often at the senior secondary, college, or university level, teaching such subjects as philosophy, science, and technology.

Like their namesake, Promethean Achievers want to make man more like the

NT

Visionaries, Architects, Builders, Competitors, Knowers

strive to be competent.

FINISH

gods. The light the NTs bring is not the light of fire, but the light of understanding. Knowledge gives the NT and those around her the ability to understand and thereby control the forces of nature, of life itself.

The NT loves intelligence. As a rule, the NT becomes a lifelong learner, and she seeks to surround herself with others who are intelligent. She is irritated by those who do not seek to educate themselves. The NT, a generous teacher, does not suffer indifference to education easily.

Impatient and sometimes too openly critical of any sign of incompetence, the NT has an unmatched drive for excellence. She is hard on others and is often resented for what often appears to be her condescending attitude.

What those being judged by the NT might want to remember is that the NT is hardest on herself. She constantly monitors her own performance and feels a compulsion to perform at only the highest level. This self-analysis and criticism may not be apparent to most onlookers. Terrified of showing any sign of incompetence, the NT prefers to hide all signs of weakness. Indeed, the NT so fears appearing stupid or foolish or incompetent, she may hold back from taking risks, immobilized by her own fear of failure. For the NT, failure can be anything less than a perfect performance.

Even at play the NT is highly competitive and must achieve excellence. Never able to relax into abandoned play, the NT is always honing her skills, taking care to make no mistakes.

The NT's love of truth and of critical analysis can often lead to an aggressive, even arrogant manner. She needs to focus her attention on developing an open and positive communication style. Once this is achieved, the NT is a brilliant teacher and an even more brilliant writer of documents, papers, articles, and books that instruct, inspire, enlighten.

Naturally critical and very demanding of others, the NT reflexively questions and challenges authority, accepted knowledge, and traditional methods of study. The SJ principal should not be surprised when the NT head of the science department challenges most ideas. It is always a professional attack, never a personal one, designed to create the best system possible.

The NT prefers a complex organizational structure with flexible, changing

Temperaments and Teaching

87

■ **E**xtraversion
■ **I**ntroversion
■ **S**ensing
■ i**N**tuition
■ **T**hinking
■ **F**eeling
■ **J**udging
■ **P**erceiving

authority based on expertise. He invented the concept of the task force. Highly theoretical and achievement-oriented, the NT's goals for education are the growth of knowledge and skills.

Demanding of himself and of others, hating to be wrong or to be thought incompetent in any way, the NT becomes highly stressed when he has made foolish mistakes. He becomes even more stressed if made to look foolish in front of others. The NT response to stress is to develop unreasonable fears and experience crippling self-doubt.

The NT appreciates being praised for his intelligence, his analytical ability and inventiveness. Wise colleagues would be careful never to ridicule the NT and often to appreciate his active and insightful imagination.

The NT lives his work and, to be happy, must succeed at it. Luckily, he usually does.

The Dionysian Free Spirit (SP)

When you combine the immediacy and practical realism of sensation with the curiosity and thirst for spontaneous experience of the perceiving function, you have a Dionysian Free Spirit, the SP temperament.

The SP is driven, above all, by the need to be free, to do what he wishes and to do it now. To do it for the sheer joy of doing it. To tell the SP to wait for tomorrow is to say "forget it," for tomorrow never comes. Focused on the present, the SP is a being of action, the person who wastes nothing, including time.

Uncomfortable with the structured and theoretical nature of higher learning, SPs are not often found in the teaching profession. Although they are 38 percent of the population, they comprise only 4 percent of

SP

Doers, Negotiators, Troubleshooters, Counselors, Performers

need to be free to do.

the teaching population and have the shortest stay in the profession (Keirsey and Bates 1978, pp. 39, 166). This is a sad loss, because many SP children find school very difficult (SPs have the highest dropout rate of all types). These SP students could benefit from the understanding an SP teacher would offer.

All ISTP, ESTP, ISFP, and ESFP types are Free Spirits. For the SP, quality is directly related to freedom to do. The duty needed by the SJ, the power craved by the NT, the spirit of enlightenment valued by the NF are secondary to the SP, who in his focus on action may go beyond any SJ in duty, any NT in power, and any NF in enlightenment. But those goals, per se, are never there.

A look at how one plays the piano is a nice way to demonstrate SP attitude. The SJ will practice his piano and become a very competent player because his mother is paying for the lessons.

The NF will practice the piano and become a moving performer because she wants to express the essence of her soul through her own interpretation of Beethoven.

The NT will practice and master the keyboard because he cannot be anything less than perfect, or he will stubbornly refuse to practice for fear of failure.

But the SP plays and plays and plays because he loves to touch his fingers to the cool clean beauty of the ivory and feel the rhythm in his bones and hear the perfect beauty of each note he plays. He becomes the Liberace, the Elvis Presley, the Pavarotti, the Picasso—the best in the world at what he does.

On the other hand, if the SP doesn't want piano lessons, or singing lessons, or violin lessons, forget it. You're wasting your money and, in the eyes of the SP, something worse. You are wasting his time and taking away a most precious commodity: his freedom to be doing other things. Things he wants to do.

The SP enjoys being impulsive, feeling guilty when he doesn't have impulses and feeling bound when he can't give in to them. This love of impulsivity, this craving to do something unplanned, leads the SP to enjoy crises, to almost crave them. An expert troubleshooter, the SP uses his sensory skills to get an immediate read on the situation and then uses his perceiving function to size up the situation and determine what is best to do right now. This troubleshooting skill makes the SP teacher a valuable member of any committee charged with negotiations.

The SP exudes an energy, a spirit, a love of life that is irresistible. This SP love of the moment makes him the king of process orientation: it is not the goal at the end of the road, but how one acts on the way that counts. This wonderful energy can give magic to any classroom, any school. It is especially important for the SJ principal not to quell this energy, not to restrict the SP who craves freedom and hates waste of time and energy. The SP does not want to be restricted by too many rules, too much red tape, too much supervision.

Intent on making space for spontaneity and freedom for himself and his students, he prefers an organizational structure that is direct and simple and practical. A friendly, hierarchical, but open structure is appreciated. He deeply resents complexity, hypocrisy, and rigidity in the organization.

Resourceful and easygoing, the SP creates classrooms that are resourceful and easygoing, with students actively involved in learning that they can see a practical use for almost immediately.

Other types may resent the SP's spirit, not really understanding his motivations. For instance, an SJ may observe the SP's remarkable endurance and focus when he is engaged in something he wants to do. The SJ may mistakenly judge these actions to be discipline, something the SJ values. The SJ then expects the SP to be disciplined forever more. You can imagine the SJ's disappointment when the SP loses interest, becomes attracted to a different action, and abandons the project at hand. The report is left on the desk, the governmental statisti-

■ **E**xtraversion

■ **I**ntroversion

■ **S**ensing

■ i**N**tuition

■ **T**hinking

■ **F**eeling

■ **J**udging

■ **P**erceiving

FIGURE II.I

The Four Temperaments in Teaching

	Traditionalist (SJ)	Change Agent (NF)	Achiever (NT)	Free Spirit (SP)
Prime value in education	growth of responsi-bility and utility	growth of identity and integrity	growth of know-ledge and skills	growth of spontan-taneity and freedom
Percentage of teachers	56%	32%	8%	4%
Length of service	long stay in teaching	long stay in teaching	medium stay in teaching	short stay in teaching
Favored teaching areas	agriculture, clerical, business, sports, social sciences, political science home, economics, history, geography	humanities, social sciences, theater, music, foreign languages, speech, theology	philosophy, science, technol-ogy, communica-tions, mathematics, linguistics	arts, crafts, sports, drama, music, recreation
Favored instructional techniques	recitation, drill composition, tests or quizzes, demonstration	group projects, interaction, discussion, shows, simulations, games	lectures, tests, compositions, projects, reports	projects, contests, games, demon-strations, shows

SOURCE: ADAPTED FROM D. KEIRSEY AND M. BATES, *PLEASE UNDERSTAND ME* (DEL MAR, CALIF.: PROMETHEUS NEMESIS BOOK CO., 1984), P. 166.

cal analysis is stuffed in the garbage, the floor is left unswept. Where is the SP? Teaching his class to skydive, putting out a fire in the drama teacher's closet, saving the school $10,000 by negotiating a great deal.

The SP can be resourceful, a fire raging with wonderful and fierce energy. The SP usually has a secret plan about what to do and how to do it and resents any interference or interruption at any level. The SP works best without her wings clipped. Appreciate her boldness, endurance, cleverness, adaptation, timing. Acknowledge that

process is as important as product. Trust her to do the job her way. Let her soar with the eagle, the bat, the butterfly. And do everything to keep her in the profession that so desperately needs her.

Magic Making

Figure 11.1 summarizes the characteristics of the four temperaments in education. You may want to bring this chart into your next staff meeting. Try to analyze the temperament needs that drive people's behavior.

When the SJ becomes overwrought with too much to do, help her by suggesting specific ways to share the responsibility. Comment on her hard work and dedication

When the NT struggles over a problem, help to supply the knowledge he needs to have to gain a sense of control over the situation. Comment on his insight.

When the NF takes a risk, pushes the envelope, support his idea, recognize his integrity and inspiration.

When the SP feels cornered by too much bureaucracy, help her to open doors, find solutions more quickly. Comment on her ability to get the job done.

For a month, consciously use your knowledge of type theory to help your colleagues. When people start feeling good and smiling a lot, you can feel the success of the magic you've begun to weave.

If you are an SJ, you may do it because you want the school to run well. It's your job to help that happen. If you are an NT, you want everyone to be as competent as possible. If this helps, why not? An NF will be most attracted to using type theory to make things better in the teachers' lounge. As an NF you are driven to make positive changes in people. If you are an SP, you'll do whatever it takes to get the show on the road. Onward and upward!

12

Don't Let the Moon Break Your Heart

This little piece first appeared in 1984 as an article in *Educational Leadership*. It has been reprinted in many other journals and has been compulsory reading in many Canadian schools. The popularity of the piece can only tell me that teachers are troubled by the learner who seems to love life and hate school. In an effort to help these students, teachers are searching for a way to bring the pleasure of living into the classroom. To that end, let me tell you the story of Mickey.

Stardust

Grade four: "Having Mickey in my class is like having ethereal stardust sprinkled everywhere. Her joy is absolutely contagious."

Any mother would be pleased to read such a comment on her child's report card. It was my daughter's fourth year in school, and she couldn't have been happier. Her teacher was alive with great ideas. She took her little friends on walks in the woods and read to them under the arms of sweet-smelling tamarack, while they nibbled ripe berries until tummies were full or branches empty.

My daughter loved this gentle, wise young woman. So did I. I was surprised when, during the year-end parent-teacher interview, the teacher suggested I send Mickey to a private school, a convent maybe, just for girls.

"What? Why?"

"I'm not sure. I just feel she has to be . . . protected, somehow."

"A convent school?" I was almost getting angry.

"I know of one north of here. The nuns are so loving. They run a farm. You learn to do so many things . . . it is really so freeing . . . "

It was out of the question. I was not ready to send my only child to a boarding school.

Not yet.

Grade ten: "Mickey is having difficulty in this class. She has missed so much school, I am unable to assign her any grade. She is so reluctant to try the assignments—how can I teach her? We can discuss this at the parent-teacher interview.

There isn't a mother alive who would have looked forward to going to that interview.

"She has failed the composition section!"

"Failed composition?" I, a Professor of English, gulped.

"She missed the whole unit on poetry."

"Have you read any of the poetry she writes?"

"She writes poetry?"

"Almost every day."

Silence.

"She didn't do any of the exercises on grammar." This grade ten teacher was persistent.

"Have you ever heard her make a grammatical error?" I wasn't ready to submit.

"I've never heard her *speak!*"

The Reluctant Learner

That some students are reluctant to learn in almost any educational environment is a painful reality for teachers, parents, and, predominantly, the learners themselves. That many of these students share a common learning style is only now being discovered by researchers (Lawrence 1979, Mamchur 1984, Myers 1980).

The basis of the learning style descriptors used by these researchers is an exami-

nation of personality constructs described by Carl Jung. Jung postulated that many apparently random differences in the way people behave are actually quite orderly and consistent, resulting from specific fundamental differences in the way people prefer to focus their energy and use perception and judgment. This system for examining individual preference variables Jung called his theory of psychological types. The major focus of Jung's theory concentrated on two fundamental human attitudes, extraversion and introversion. In the extraverted attitude, attention flows outward, toward the objects and people of the environment. Associated with this energy flow is a desire to act on the environment, to affirm its importance, to increase the effect of the environment on the extravert.

In the introverted attitude, energy seems to flow inward, back to the subject, who conserves this energy and uses it to examine his or her own ideas and concepts and reaffirm or dispel them. The introverted attitude is reflective in nature; the extraverted is active.

Jung further defined his system in terms of four functions: sensing, intuition, thinking, and feeling. Sensing and intuition are the two basic processes of becoming aware of things or people or occurrences or ideas. Thinking and feeling are the two basic processes of coming to conclusions about what has been perceived. Sensing is the process that establishes what exists. It is the practical, straightforward perception that relies on the five senses to provide information. Intuition refers to the use of insight to see possibilities and relationships. Thinking is the judging function that links ideas together in an objective, logical, analytical fashion. Feeling, also a judging function, arranges ideas together in an

Don't Let the Moon Break Your Heart ■ **E**xtraversion

■ **I**ntroversion

93 ■ **S**ensing

■ i**N**tuition

■ **T**hinking

■ **F**eeling

■ **J**udging

■ **P**erceiving

equally rational but subjective manner according to the value system of the person making the decision. Jung defined these functions as "particular forms of psychic activity that remain the same in principle under varying conditions" (Jung 1971 {originally published 1921}, p. 436). It is this concept that makes understanding psychological types so useful to educators. Learning styles can be understood by using the Jungian system as a framework for observing student behavior.

One further explanation postulated by Jung is that an individual, because of an inborn predisposition comes to favor one of the four functions of sensing, intuition, thinking, or feeling in the course of normal development. That favored function is considered the *dominant* one, the most interesting and most rewarding of the mental processes.

Myers (1962) has further used this classification of dominant function as a means of explaining how individuals interact with the environment. Those folks who use sensing or intuition as a favorite function for dealing with the environment are categorized as *perceiving* types. Those who prefer the environmental interface of thinking or feeling are labeled *judging* types. Each type has distinct attributes. The outstanding and much admired quality of perceiving types is their flexibility, curiosity, receptiveness, spontaneity, and adaptability to change. For judging types it is a sense of decisiveness, responsibility and order, and a willingness to apply oneself to tasks and to have long-range plans for the future.

The Sensing Perceiving (SP) Type

Several longitudinal studies (Keirsey and Bates 1978, McCaulley 1977, Myers 1976)

show that those students preferring the *sensing* way of functioning and the *perceiving* way of interfacing with the environment seem the most resistant to institutional learning. These students have a combination of sensing and perceiving attributes. The sensing attributes commonly seen are:

• A love for fact
• A need for relevancy
• An appreciation of the practical
• A tendency to cling to the certainty of actual things
• A materialism
• A preference to focus on the here and now

The perceiving attributes commonly seen are:

• A love for the spontaneous
• A dislike of time schedules
• A need for a release from the rigidity of rules, of patterns, of constant, fixed ways of organizing their lives
• A desire to be aware of process
• A reluctance to take initiative in decision making
• A flexibility in attitude
• A tendency to leave things to the last minute
• A love for surprise

Of all students, the highest drop-out rate can be found among sensing-perceiving (SP) learners. Only 1 percent of teachers are SP, however. This type, in contrast to all others, is relatively unmotivated by long-term goals. Instead, SP people are driven by a need to be free, free to do whatever they wish, whenever they wish. The overall goal of the SP is freedom—not freedom as an end, or as a means to an end, but freedom for its own sake. There is, essentially, no purpose in life; there is only being. This most process-oriented type acts on impulse, not design. The goal, then, is to have no goal. The king of whim and whimsy, the SP is a follower of Dionysus, god of music, song, and dance, god of joy.

SP types can become great performing artists. They play musical instruments or sing, for example, not to become great, but to *do*. And by doing, become great. Becoming great is not the goal, simply a pleasant side effect of the endless pursuit of doing, doing, and doing again.

Lock such a freedom-oriented being into a structure and the result is a natural resistance and resentment powerful enough to prevent learning. The SP becomes labeled as dumb, stubborn, lazy, even insane. If the SP child is extraverted, hyperactivity is often apparent. The introverted SP, on the other hand, is markedly withdrawn.

To teach such children is at best frustrating. To mother such a child can often be heartbreaking. I have spoken to many such mothers. I am one. My daughter, Mickey, is an introverted SP. She started "withdrawing" from regular school in kindergarten, even though she could read when she was four years old. By the tenth grade it was all I could do to coax Mickey to attend guitar class for one hour twice a week with a teacher she especially liked. School had become unbearable.

Today she is attending a Quaker boarding school in the heart of the mountains, beside the loveliest river in British Columbia. In this school freedom, responsibility, and relevance are key words. The school is small, intimate, community centered. The students are as responsible as the adults for maintaining, even building, the school.

Even in this ideal and idyllic setting, where flexibility and freedom to do (two absolute musts for the SP child) are afforded the student, my daughter and three other SP students have difficulty. But they are surviving, they are learning, and slowly they are coming to be understood.

Understanding becomes a key issue in using knowledge of learning style to help the reluctant learner. Even for the learners themselves to understand "why they are so different" eases a lot of tension and self-doubt. Acceptance—on the part of the student and the teacher—can then occur. Adjustments and concessions must be made by both parties engaging in this social contract we call schooling.

But understanding does not come easy. It is human nature to expect others to behave the way we do. It finally dawned on me, when presented with the prospect of writing this paper, to ask my daughter about her learning preferences. I asked her two questions:

1. What do you like about English class?

2. What do you dislike?

These are her exact words; her voice trembled as she spoke. "In school I *hate* . . ." (I had not mentioned hating, I had asked about liking) "In school I *hate* doing ridiculous things that don't make any sense. I hate essays, all those rambling ideas, demands of 'show the significance of this, relate this to that.' I *hate* it!" (It is an interesting fact that most English teachers are intuitive types. Intuitives value the world of possibility, of relationships, of hypothesis.) She continued, "I hate school. This is true. I hate school. And I hate intuitive things. Let me be more specific," she added in true sensing fashion. "Hold on, let me think. I don't like teaching that goes on and on, that demands we go behind a thing, to find the secret meaning. I mean, it is what it is. I wish teachers would let it go at that." (Sensing types are realists. Intuitives are

Don't Let the Moon Break Your Heart

95

■ **E**xtraversion
■ **I**ntroversion
■ **S**ensing
■ i**N**tuition
■ **T**hinking
■ **F**eeling
■ **J**udging
■ **P**erceiving

dreamers.) And finally she added, "The last thing that I hate about school is scheduled things. I hate timetables, doing the same thing everyday. I hate that."

And indeed, true to her type Mickey wanted unscheduled, nonintuitive, relevant, specific, here-and-now learning.

It was more difficult to coax from her what she *liked* about the English class. Finally, she admitted, "In English class I like discussing things that are really relevant, like the situation in El Salvador. Going on the peace march to Washington, now that made sense. I like one-word answer tests, match and mismatch. I like ABC choices. Not those damn questions that have 40 possible answers." (All of these were typical preferences of the practical, realistic, fact-oriented sensing type). "And mostly I like to go with the flow, do what we want, not have all the tasks predetermined. If something comes up, go for it." (This third point I could understand. Even though I am an intuitive type myself, I can appreciate the natural and powerful dynamic involved in the teaching moment. The SP not only appreciates it, but is starved without it). "And fourth, Mom, I like to know what's happening." "Where?" I asked, not quite sure what she meant.

"Everywhere. In class, in the world everywhere." (It was a combination of a plea for relevance and a request to be *in on the process*. She wanted to be free to observe the process, to be aware of what was happening because that is how she learns best.)

And finally, she added, "I guess I like reading a story and answering specific questions or discussing the story."

"Discussing?" I asked, surprised, knowing my daughter's introversion and reluctance to speak out in class.

"Yes, I like to *listen*."

That aspect of discussion had never occurred to the extravert in me. If one doesn't participate in the discussion, one isn't learning, right? Wrong. The introverted SP loves to be actively involved in the process of relevant discussion by listening, by observing.

"But how do you learn?" I asked, still not hearing, still not believing what my child and my understanding of typology were telling me.

"Mom, I am a good listener. I am a good observer. I'm not being a space cadet in the corner."

I guess the question I was really asking was, "How will your teacher know you are learning?"

"She could ask me."

"Ask me." It was true. That had not occurred to me either. It probably occurs to few teachers. I was learning something very important about the nature of participation for the introverted SP learner. And about the nature of trust.

Mickey and I continued our discussion on learning in the English classroom. I had to push both her and myself to discover how the SP child would know whether or not she was learning. It was easy, we discovered, when it came to skills. She could read, she could play the guitar. Even attitudes were relatively easy to assess, eventually becoming apparent from her actions. But what about her ability to understand concepts? That one perplexed me. "How do you know you are understanding the significance, for example, of a poem?"

"I just know," Mickey replied, "from the questions that run through my head. I know that if I am confused, if I don't have enough facts, that I should listen, and think of questions I would ask, and then wait for them to be answered . . . questions like, 'Who is that? What does this have to do with that?' If they aren't answered, if I am thoroughly confused, I check it out."

And suddenly, for the first time, after having studied and taught typology for years, I finally truly understood what I myself meant when I said, "Extraverts learn by talking to others; introverts talk inside their heads." Participation suddenly took on a new meaning. Introverts resent that participation "counts" because quiet participation doesn't count. Only the kind the teacher can see or hear counts. The fine tuning isn't there.

And suddenly I realized that like all other teaching tools, knowledge of learning style can work only if other qualities of good teaching are also prevalent. To truly internalize the nature of students' learning styles—especially when they are opposite to one's own—demands a big change in the teacher's attitudes. Many components of good teaching are precursors to adaptive use of learning style. In this particular instance regarding participation by an introverted student, successful teaching is incumbent on trust, empathy, and large-goal orientation. It demands positive regard. And, perhaps, it relies ultimately on an understanding of typology to make an already good situation better, a deeper understanding more possible.

What School Must Be

School must become, for the SP child, "a place to learn." Simply so. Less is more. We must provide a stimulating, relevant environment, full of important, factual things to see and hear and smell and taste and touch.

We must provide opportunity to move and act and be. And we must allow the SP to observe and enter into the process as he or she feels a need to, permitting the SP to decide when that is.

It is important to remember that SP learners cannot sit for long hours in straight rows of desks, memorizing lists of spelling words so that one day they might be successful in writing a job application. SP learners value activity, risk, and adventure. They need to be spontaneous, able to do the unexpected. Drama, visual aids, videotapes—anything appealing to the senses appeals to the SPs. They follow impulse rather than well-laid plans. They love things—things to do, things to make, things to touch, things to keep. And finally and most important, teachers must remember to keep in mind that SPs are often misunderstood and undervalued by themselves, their peers, their parents, and their teachers.

I have spoken and worked with too many SP adults who have been strapped in school, who have hidden in empty garages rather than go to school, who have been transferred from school to school, who have finally withdrawn or were expelled. I have worked in therapy with extraverted SPs who received shock treatment because they were diagnosed as mad. Some appear in juvenile court for repeated acts of stealing. These acts perplex everyone involved. The extraverted SP can display such an unconscious simultaneous love for things, such a sense of impulsive, immediate need that material things are "borrowed" and then promptly forgotten. This becomes a conundrum so complex as to go beyond the limits of this paper. It is enough to say that the ramifications of individual differences must be explored from a vantage point of under-

■ **E**xtraversion
■ **I**ntroversion
■ **S**ensing
■ i**N**tuition
■ **T**hinking
■ **F**eeling
■ **J**udging
■ **P**erceiving

standing and acceptance before growth has a chance. On a less devastating, but almost equally perplexing note, is the hyperactivity of extraverted SPs. They can be constant movers—jiggling, wiggling, jumping, talking, disturbing ad infinitum. Teachers have reported to me such events as the extraverted SP who actually rocked her desk into such motion that it broke into splinters, crashing the agitated occupant to the floor. I have been told of such students being tied to their desks, of being put into large cardboard boxes to "temper" their natures.

What a tragedy when a response to a need for movement is forced confinement. How much easier to work *with* the energy instead of against it. The extraverted SP needs large, small, and in-between body movement. Action is the key. Every opportunity to move must be not only allowed, but created. To learn to write the letter A, an extraverted SP six-year-old needs not only to sit quietly at a desk, pencil in hand. He needs to get up to the board and write A 40 times, moving across the entire expanse of the blackboard. He needs to make A's out of clay and sand and wood and cardboard, molding and shaping and sawing and hammering and cutting and pasting. He needs to tramp an A in the snow with his feet. He needs to find an A in the alphabet box and hand it to the teacher.

Extraverted SPs who love material things should be encouraged to collect stamps, records, dolls—a surfeit of things should surround little SP consumers. They can be taught to collect and trade items, to make the things they like.

This plea goes beyond a desire to keep SP students out of juvenile courts, out of cardboard boxes, out of quiet corners. Making things may "slow down" the anx-

ious collector to appreciate the product a bit more. It must be remembered that it is in the nature of this child to want things immediately. Let SPs collect bubble gum covers and you will find them buying whole cartons of bubble gum at a time. I have seen my daughter spend every cent of her allowance on a carton of such foul-tasting candy that she threw it out, stacked the coveted paper cards in a drawer, and, having collected them all in one fell swoop, promptly forgot them! Finally, I must add my belief that if "stealing" is part of the SP's pattern, the only way to teach society's system of ownership is to abandon negativity, judgment, and punishment, and replace it with patience, understanding, and acceptance of a different perspective, a different view of the way things are.

Of all types, the SP is the most joyful, the most full of spontaneous pleasure. "Look at the rainbow," says my daughter, and I search for a hidden pot of gold. She sees the glorious color of sky, now. For the SP, *now* is all there is, or need be. And in the easy acceptance and appreciation of the immediate comes a silent promise of tomorrow, simply understood and simply accepted. Uncomplicated, real, pleasure-loving, eager to do, impossible to be bound, these seekers of freedom can become the most entertaining and psychologically attractive, healthy members of any classroom. They can become magical.

> . . . Beware! Beware!
> His flashing eyes, his floating hair!
> Weave a circle round him thrice,
> And close your eyes with holy dread,
> For he on honey-dew had fed,
> And drunk the milk of Paradise.
>
> —Samuel Taylor Coleridge
> from "Kubla Khan"

References

Jung, C. (1971, originally published 1921). "Psychological Types." In *The Collected Works of C.G. Jung, Vol. 6.* Edited by R.F.C. Hull. Princeton, N.J.: Princeton University Press.

Keirsey, D., and M. Bates. (1978). *Please Understand Me.* Del Mar: Prometheus Nemesis Books.

Lawrence, G. (1979). *People Types and Tiger Stripes.* Gainesville: Center for Applications of Psychological Type (CAPT).

McCaulley, M. (1977). *The Myers Longitudinal Medical Study, Monograph 11.* Gainesville, Fla.: CAPT.

Mamchur, C. (1984). *Insights: Understanding Yourself and Others.* Toronto: Ontario Institute for Studies in Education Press.

Myers, I. (1976). "Relation of Psychological Type to Drop-Out Rate in Nursing." Preliminary Research Report. Gainesville, Fla.: CAPT.

Myers, I. (1980). *Gifts Differing.* Palo Alto, Calif.: Consulting Psychologists Press.

Myers, I. (1962). *The Myers-Briggs Type Indicator.* Princeton: Educating Testing Service.

13

Poor Uncle Harry

This chapter is adapted from an article that originally appeared in an issue of *The Journal of Experiential Education** dedicated to multicultural issues. The essence of what I say in the piece isn't about skin, color, or religion. But it could have been. All the same principles apply. "Poor Uncle Harry" speaks to the tension and vulnerability and pain associated with racism and prejudice and labeling. That is why I include it in this book.

All labeling has the potential for damage or for offering healing understanding.

As usual, I write from the inside. This chapter is really a story. My story. A story with a lesson. This chapter is about my white, middle-class Uncle Harry and his well-educated, white, middle-class niece. Me.

Grad Class

Our class was meeting once again, sharing stories, sharing food. The class had officially ended in March, and here it was August and we were still at it. I guess we didn't like endings much. I talked across the table to John, listening to his description of a great book he was recommending. We had been book traders for years, since he had taken an undergrad course with me in 1979.

Kathy was telling Donita about an article on feminist writers she'd had published in a woman's journal, and Donita was saying the highlight of her summer had been sleeping in a tent in her mother's back yard. Donita, a single parent, is the mother of a two-year-old.

As was usual for our group, we flipped from topic to topic, sharing our wins, our failures, the private ins and outs of our daily lives.

---

*C. Mamchur, "Poor Uncle Harry," *The Journal of Experiential Education* 15, 3 (November 1992): 46–50.

Jo and Jill were debating their learning style and how it affected their response to criticism. We had used Jung's theory of psychological type differences to label our learning patterns (Lawrence 1982).

In Jung's system, Jo was a "thinking" type. According to Jung, she was not supposed to mind criticism, provided it led to her being more competent.

"I hate labels," I half heard her say. "'Thinkers' sounds so stuffy and uptight." It was interesting that Jo, very Italian, had come from a family where emotions were highly valued. Cool logic was not.

"'Feelers' sounds so gushy and dumb." Donita threw in her ten cents' worth. She was feeling a bit left out. She had never published a piece, even though she was a good writer.

I could feel the energy move my way. I knew we'd be discussing "labels" in a few minutes. I glanced at Kathy. She and Donita were still heavy into Kathy's publishing exploits. Kathy's face glowed with the excitement and joy of a young woman proud of a recent accomplishment.

"God, I wish I looked like you," I blurted out. Kathy blushed. I could have said, "You're beautiful." Instead I said, "God, I wish I looked like you." I don't know where the words came from. Everyone looked at Kathy. "Nobody has ever said that to me," Kathy replied as she blushed an even deeper red, down into her throat the way she did when she was really excited, embarrassed, or pleased.

Everyone began to agree with me. They began to comment on Kathy's thick auburn hair, the glow she carried, how wonderfully she wore blue. And purple. And gold. How her smile made you want to hug her.

Would Kathy have liked to be labeled "beautiful?" I wondered, as we raved on about her Irish beauty. My guess was that the feminist in her would not believe in "beautiful" even though she was. She wouldn't believe in the idea of labeling someone as beautiful because "we are all beautiful in our way," "beauty is in the eye of the beholder," "if one person is beautiful, is another who doesn't look that way, not beautiful?"

Yet, she was beautiful. And we could all agree on it. When somebody is a whole lot of a thing, it's pretty easy to recognize. Especially when the notion of "beauty" is common knowledge to the group—beauty in every connotation, from the television stereotype to the platonic and Romantic philosophical interpretation.

Any descriptor, I suppose, can become a label. And it can be misused.

"Would we label Kathy beautiful?" I asked. Jo smiled.

"I still hate labels," she assured me.

"Wouldn't you say they're dangerous?" Jill wanted to know. Everyone looked at me this time.

They wanted to discuss the system we had been using, a system I had taught them that essentially "labeled" people as certain types.

As I often do, I turned to that method taught to me one July afternoon by that great teacher Paulo Freire: I told a story.

"I'm not sure," I said, "Sometimes. Let me tell you about my Uncle Harry. Maybe that will help."

Everyone sat back, sipped wine, finished dessert.

The Women in Our Family

Most of the women on my mother's side of the family could be accused of a healthy

Poor Uncle Harry ■ **Extraversion**

101 ■ **Introversion**

■ **Sensing**

■ **iNtuition**

■ **Thinking**

■ **Feeling**

■ **Judging**

■ **Perceiving**

aggression. I've heard it said the characteristic has served us well. Although born in a small prairie town of immigrant parents, most of my mother's sisters and aunts and cousins and nieces became lawyers or accountants or aldermen or business women or brokers or nursing administrators. I've also heard it said it hasn't been too easy on the men in our lives.

I know for sure none of us was very easy on my Uncle Harry. "Poor Uncle Harry," we'd say, "he just isn't too good at business." My aunt would get him started in one, and pretty soon she'd be running it and Uncle Harry would be helping.

When Uncle Harry came to visit he'd sit quietly on the edges of things—couches, dining room tables, lawn furniture, conversations—seemingly uninterested in the latest adventure my aunt and mom were discussing in excited, laughing voices or intense, conspiratorial whispers. As a young girl, I loved being around my mom and her sister. They were so intense and happy and busy. Life was always interesting when you were near them.

My Uncle Harry made me feel rather nervous. He was so quiet, and he seemed to watch everything so carefully, especially me. When he spoke to me it was as if he knew exactly what I was thinking, as if he had been watching and thinking about me for a long time. I didn't like it. The older I got, the more I didn't like it.

Sadly, I had reason to know what it can sometimes mean to have an older male family member look at you too closely, to talk to you in a soft, knowing voice. Sadly, too, at that age I thought I knew what I had to do. I had to keep it a secret, and I had to keep away from my Uncle Harry.

I did keep away from him. We never really talked, never really engaged in any meaningful way, until my mother died. My aunt, ever the supporter, ever the organizer, came to help me. Uncle Harry came with her.

A Closer Look

To disperse of my mother's belongings, I invited our relatives and friends to take anything in her house that they might want to have. I was surprised when my Uncle Harry asked if I would mind his taking a painting I had done for my mother when I was a girl. "I remember when you painted it," he said, "and how pleased your mother was." He wanted an old kerosene lamp he remembered from my grandmother's kitchen on the farm and a deck of cards from the days he and my grandfather had played cribbage.

He spent time with me that week telling me about the father who had left when I was a baby. He told me how funny my father had been, funny and generous and handsome. I had never heard those things said about my father before.

"He stole money out of my bank account when he left," I protested. "And I was only two."

"I know. It was the damn booze," Uncle Harry sighed. "You know he gave up his weekend off in the fall of '44, filled in for me before he was sent overseas, so I could be with your aunt when our first baby was born. He could have been charged if anyone had found out he'd changed places with me."

I didn't give much thought to how my Uncle Harry knew I needed to hear good things about my father at that time, but he was right. I did.

My uncle and aunt stayed on for a while. "Just for a holiday," they said. I was grateful. As an only child suddenly finding myself parentless, I was feeling pretty alone, pretty abandoned.

My Uncle Harry retreated into his usual watchful silence, and I began to grow uncomfortable with it again. No longer afraid of molestation, I was now an ardent opponent to any hint of sexual abuse. I was especially watchful of how my uncle seemed so pleased around my daughter, Mickey.

Mickey never mentioned any sense of discomfort. But then, my daughter was always pretty quiet about things. "What do you think of my Uncle Harry?" I asked her, trying to hide the worry in my voice. "I like him." she said "He's the only relative we have who's just like me."

"Like you?"

Mickey smiled. "Sure, short and sweet."

Uncle Harry was a good three inches over six feet tall. He probably weighed in at two hundred and forty pounds. I frowned.

"I mean, I think he's my type." Mickey patted my stupid head.

Psychological Type

Type theory grows out of the work of Jung (1971, originally published 1921) and Myers (1962). Jung was very driven to create a practical psychology that would help individuals understand one another. He decided the best way to create an understandable map of the mind would be to simplify human behavior into different identifiable categories. He called these categories psychological types.

His first simplification was to divide all human behavior into two component parts: perception and judgment. He claimed you must choose between the open act of perceiving or finding out and the closed act

of judging or deciding or taking action. It is theoretically impossible to do both simultaneously.

Adding up all the mental decisions to either perceive or judge results in a preference. Jung further maintained that individuals prefer to perceive through either their senses or their intuition, and they prefer to make judgments through either feeling or thinking. Although all four functions of sensing, intuition, feeling, and thinking are present in every individual, Jung insisted that one is dominant and serves the individual best; one is auxiliary, used to balance the dominant function; the third is tertiary and is less often exercised and demands more energy to use; the fourth is a person's inferior function—the person's weak spot.

The final dimension of Jung's theory is extraversion and introversion. Those people who get energy and excitement and satisfaction from external forces in the world around them are extraverts. They will extravert their dominant or favorite function.

Introverts, on the other hand, look to internal resources as a source of energy and satisfaction and safety. They introvert, or internalize, their dominant function and are less easy to understand than extraverts. With an extravert you "see what you get." With an introvert you must look a bit more carefully. An introvert might offer the warmth of a fur coat, but the fur is on the inside.

All this theory became accessible to the public when Isabel Myers published the Myers-Briggs Type Indicator in 1962.

I began to get the picture. According to the system based on an analysis of personality preferences (described by Jung as psychological type theory), my daughter is described as an introverted feeling type who uses sensation as an auxiliary function.

■ **E**xtraversion

■ **I**ntroversion

■ **S**ensing

■ **i**N**t**uition

■ **T**hinking

■ **F**eeling

■ **J**udging

■ **P**erceiving

How this translates into everyday language is that my daughter's introversion results in her being thoughtful, reflective, loyal, sensitive, soft-spoken. She appears shy and withdrawn and is rather unobtrusive and very introspective. Her most trusted way of dealing with the world is her feeling, and this preference results in clear, strong convictions, a high need for harmony, a great deal of empathy, and a marvelously accepting attitude toward people--unless of course, they expect her to go against her own beliefs.

Mickey's preference for sensation results in a love of things, of sights, sounds, tastes, smells. She has a remarkable interest in and memory for detail, particularly when it relates to people. Her favorite activity is people watching.

My daughter has certainly broken the pattern of being an aggressive woman in our family. She is soft-spoken, and has consistently avoided formal education. That avoidance started in kindergarten. Understanding psychological type theory has helped me to understand her. And it has helped me learn how not to drive both of us crazy with worry.

Learning what was natural and happy and satisfying for my daughter helped us both (see Chapter 12). When I met happy, successful adults who shared her orientations for introversion, sensing, feeling, and perception (ISFP), I said out loud, "Thank you, God."

Over the years, through interviews and phone calls and much research, I learned that people of Mickey's psychological type preference are natural observers, keen to experience adventure and spontaneous interaction; they are unwilling to endure the routine regimentation, lack of meaningful interaction, and slow rewards of formal

education. Happily, I learned that they often grow up to be volunteers, parents, adventurers, negotiators, nurses, counselors, teachers, artists, gardeners. I learned that they are loving, generous, free spirits who rejoice in everyday life in a way few of us ever experience.

Knowing these facts helped us through the terrible twelves—twelve years of school, that is. In the process I came to understand and accept and love all the personality characteristics that had at times frustrated and confused me.

When Mickey suggested Uncle Harry was "like her," I donned my "psychological type" reading glasses and suddenly I could see the fine print of my uncle's personality that I had missed before.

A Really Close Look

Old misconceptions disappeared. I saw Uncle Harry's tendency to look closely at things for what it was: careful, concerned observation. His ability to remember details about everything around him, his need to relate intimately, if shyly, became endearing, nonthreatening qualities to be cherished and enjoyed. When I started to share my new understandings with him, he laughed and asked me if I would like him to complete the Myers-Briggs Type Indicator, the instrument developed by Isabel Myers to determine psychological type preferences. I was delighted.

Over the next three weeks, while drinking his morning coffee, Uncle Harry answered the 126 questions that constitute the Myers-Briggs Type Indicator. He answered only a few each day, but he did it. He even read sections of Myers's (1980) wonderful book *Gifts Differing*. He told me that reading the book made him feel happy. I scored his answers as he and my daughter read selections from *Insights,* my book on psychological type designed for lay readers (see Mamchur 1984b). They laughed at my stories, my explanations of human behavior.

Sure enough, he was the same type as my daughter, Mickey. As I watched them hug in delight and conspiratorial recognition, I felt a familiar pang of guilt and anger. I recognized, in his inability to "perform" in ways other family members considered important, my own daughter's struggle with a society unable to adapt to her particular learning style. Natural artists, performers, athletes . . . this type excels for the love of it! They excel, that is, provided they are lucky enough to find the area that's right for them. If not, they search for a way to be active and free, motivating others to seek what is abundant and joyful in life.

My uncle, often forced into many fields, had struggled, but had not found his niche. He was not alone. His and my daughter's type, the ISFP, has a high drop-out rate in school and a low success rate in rigid business. Natural therapists, they are rarely found in the counseling field because of the long, and to them, often unrelated-to-the-job early training period. Attracted to working with others, they often begin on the job, offering volunteer services and sometimes working their way up, taking night courses directly related to what they are doing, until they earn a real position of responsibility. My uncle had not been one of those lucky ones.

Saying Good-bye

The year I really "met" my Uncle Harry, we also learned he was dying of lung cancer. One of his many jobs had been to work the mines in Northern Manitoba.

That final year we became very close. In fact, next to my daughter, he became my favorite relative. I had the chance to confess my unfair, early reaction to him. I even explained my awful bias and talked about the sexual abuse I had suffered as a child.

My uncle was sympathetic and caring. Despite his shyness, he confided in me that through our discussion about type, for the first time ever, he felt truly understood by a family member. Losing him was a terrible sorrow, a terrible loss. I couldn't imagine that just one year before, I might have said, "Poor Uncle Harry" and gone on with my life. My sense of loss meant, at least for a little while, I had been close to my favorite uncle.

Uncle Eaters

My grad class listened, nodded, filled my glass with wine. Together we decided labels can be terrible things and useful things. They help us perceive based on a set of data. If the data include a bad past experience, like sexual abuse, we may wrongly view the world. If the data include a set of descriptors that help us to understand someone who seems different from us, and perhaps confusing or frustrating or even frightening, the labels help us to get things straight.

One set of labels had made a prisoner of me and of many others too. People of my generation watched World War II movies which insisted the Japanese were treacherous and would sneak out of wet places in the middle of the night to capture and torture. We heard phrases such as "that's white of you," "Jew him down," "That's just the Irish in her."

Today, we are more aware of such biases in conversation. I hope awareness will free us from our storehouse of prejudices.

■ **E**xtraversion

■ **I**ntroversion

■ **S**ensing

■ **iN**tuition

■ **T**hinking

■ **F**eeling

■ **J**udging

■ **P**erceiving

Free both sides, the hater and the hated. No one could deny the anger and terror and frustration so many blacks have suffered because of prejudice. Only recently has there been a growing awareness of how prejudice affects the person with the prejudice. Imagine the emotional turmoil of a white person living in Georgia who believes all blacks are dangerous. She must also feel in danger. I have noticed the triple-edged sword of prejudice appearing in British Columbia. An influx of people from Hong Kong has resulted in a wave of anger and resentment and fear on the part of Vancouver's citizens. Third generation Chinese are suddenly feeling a part of the "yellow enemy, bringing gangs, drug money, escalated prices."

As the world gets smaller, instead of merging, people too often tend to get tighter, more protective, more fearful. "They are cutting down all the trees to build big houses," "They are increasing the insurance rates with their bad driving" is the new language of prejudice. This time, the fear is not based on war or poverty. It is based on power and money. But the consequences are very similar. Prejudice attacks the innocent and separates people. It eats peace of mind. It steals uncles. And none of us is free of it. None of us.

Our Conclusions

It is our responsibility to use all labels wisely, to examine our own biases, our motives, the accuracy of our data. Is our system of labeling helpful to our understanding? If not, can we let it go? Can anything or anyone help us?

Ironically, a second kind of label had set me free. The use of labels or criteria or systems to understand people, no longer the domain of psychologists and educators, has permeated all aspects of everyday living. The terms coined by Carl Jung to explain psychological traits such as extraversion and introversion have, 50 years later, become almost household terms.

As a group of educators/writers who use psychological type theory as a daily part of our work in teaching, consulting, and writing, we recognize again the power, for good and harm, of using a set of descriptors to interpret behavior. We work continually at ridding ourselves of hurtful biases so they no longer cloud our vision of our world. We study what we perceive to be useful, clarifying systems to help us in the process. We agreed psychological type theory is the best system we had found so far.

It is also the only system that we have found to be "culture free." Translated into other languages, the wording of the questions changes, but the concepts, the descriptors run true across all cultures. No one culture is, for example, more extraverted or introverted than any other culture. Jung claimed the archetypal nature of type was responsible for its lack of bias. "Archetypes are without known origin, and they reproduce themselves in any time or in any part of the world" (Jung 1964).

The use of psychological type in the world of health, industry, and education is spreading rapidly, and I, for one, am grateful. We seem to need all the help we can get.

"Oh, okay. Kathy is beautiful," Jo said, smiling. "And I am a thinking type."

We toasted ourselves and called it a night.

"Same time next week?" John asked.

"I'll have to bring my kid," Donita warned.

"Sounds good to me."

References

Jung, C. (1964). *Man and His Symbols*. Garden City, N.Y.: Doubleday.

Jung, C. (1971, originally published 1921). "Psychological Types." In *The Collected Works of C.G. Jung, Vol. 6*. Princeton, N.J.: Princeton University Press.

Lawrence, G. (1982). *People Types and Tiger Stripes*. Gainesville, Fla.: Center for Applications of Psychological Type.

Mamchur, C. (1984a). "Don't Let the Moon Break Your Heart." *Educational Leadership* 41, 5: 76–83. *Note:* This article is reprinted as Chapter 12 in this book.

Mamchur, C. (1984b). *Insights: Understanding Yourself and Others*. Toronto: Ontario Institute for Studies in Education Press.

Myers, I. (1962). *The Myers-Briggs Type Indicator*. Palo Alto, Calif.: Consulting Psychologists Press.

Myers, I. (1980). *Gifts Differing*. Palo Alto, Calif.: Consulting Psychologists Press.

P.S.
Thank You,
Mrs. Farnell

Though most authors resist the temptation to add a postscript to their work, I would guess that they have the unspoken urge to add something, especially as the words go to the printer.

I have never been good at resisting temptation. I have just one more thing to say, one more story to tell.

This book has focused on the importance of knowing and applying learning style theory, yet I feel compelled to remind the reader that it is not the ability to design curriculum according to Jungian type codes that separates the great teachers from the not-so-great ones.

Learning style applications can add to excellence, can guide the teacher toward greater awareness and understanding, but they can never be a substitute for the most important aspect of teaching: the teacher's perception of her relationship with her students.

Let me tell you the story of a teacher who never consciously considered learning style theory. Permit me to tell you the story of Mrs. Farnell.

It was my first year of teaching and I wanted to be just like her, Mrs. Farnell, my grade 9 teacher. She was the best teacher I'd ever had. Everyone in her class always passed. I remember the day she told us the average grade for our class was 89 percent. We looked around at ourselves in amazement, with more than a little pride. She thanked us all for working so hard. I remember that I felt like thanking her for working so hard. Maybe somebody did. I know we felt like a team.

I guess it was natural for me to want to imitate her. I'll never forget the first time I tried. The students in my grade 10 literature

---

Adapted, with permission, from "Thank You, Mrs. Farnell," *Teaching and Learning* 3, 3 (Spring 1989): 49–51.

class were not paying the slightest attention to me. I had gone to all the trouble of memorizing Antony's speech at Julius Caesar's funeral. I was delivering it with all the passion a 20-year-old body could muster, and those little monkeys were passing notes, catching up on their math homework, or daydreaming. Right in the middle of my "Friends, Romans, country-men" speech, I decided to turn into Mrs. Farnell. Whenever we had misbehaved in her class, she would close her Latin text, sit at her desk, take out a library book, and begin to read to herself. A hush would fall across the room. "If you don't want to learn, I'd rather not try to teach," she'd say. My God! We'd beg her to continue, ashamed at how we'd insulted or offended someone we all respected so much. "Okay," she'd say, and the lesson would go on with 35 blushing but attentive faces focused on her.

Well, it had worked for her. I stopped reciting. I sat at my desk and opened *Anna Karenina.* I began to read to myself.

"What are you doing?" one student shouted.

"Is it silent reading now?"

"No," I responded, a bit miffed at the lack of hushed silence. "No," I continued in my calm, Mrs. Farnell voice," if you don't want to learn, then I shan't teach."

The cheers of "Yippee" and "Yay," the wild tossing of books in the air, and the sudden burst of exuberant energy for talking and goofing off turned me from being miffed to bewildered to despairing. I rushed from the room and sobbed to the silent sickly yellow walls of the girl's washroom. A Mrs. Farnell I was not!

With the painful lessons of experience, I developed my own style. Demure sophistication and old-world gentility were not to

be my forte. Mrs. Farnell was a woman who served tea with lemon slices on bone china in a room decorated with Queen Anne furniture and daffodils. I was more of a pillows on the floor and a wild array of red poppies type. I learned to use humor and field trips to win the hearts and minds of my students.

What was it, then, that had so attracted me to Mrs. Farnell? Why did she, over the years, continue to be the ideal which flashed its lights in my brain cells every time I wanted to "do it right"?

Mrs. Farnell taught me the essentials of good teaching. I sensed this before I was actually able to recognize what those qualities were. In my eagerness and youth I had mistaken her methods for the essentials, and I had passed right by the good stuff, the real stuff.

I'm afraid much of the research and analysis on teacher effectiveness does the same thing. It focuses on process and product.

But do these researchers have the experience, the insight, to recognize the real attributes of successful teaching? What would the teacher effectiveness experts see in Mrs. Farnell?

For sure they would note that the class average was 89 percent. They could note her time on task and her clarity in giving instructions and making expectations known.

And 8,000,000 teachers could strive to have their students earn high grades, stay focused, understand information, and know what was expected of them. But would doing so make these teachers a "Mrs. Farnell" type teacher? Unfortunately, probably not.

It wasn't what she did; it was what she

■ **E**xtraversion

■ **I**ntroversion

■ **S**ensing

■ i**N**tuition

■ **T**hinking

■ **F**eeling

■ **J**udging

■ **P**erceiving

believed about herself and us that made her a great teacher.

She believed we were trustworthy and able. She identified with us, treating us with the same respect she expected from us. She cared about us as people. She fit perfectly Arthur Combs's description of effective professional helpers: those who feel identified with the student, rather than against; who care about the student on a personal, rather than an impersonal, level; who are concerned with large goals and issues, rather than small, immediate behavioral objectives; and who perceive the student as able, rather than unable or indifferent (Combs 1965, 1982).

How would a researcher observe these beliefs in Mrs. Farnell's behavior? They would hear her asking us how much homework we had done and if we felt we needed more or less, and they would observe her acting on our responses.

They would see her writing notes to us on scented stationery whenever we won an award or sang a song or represented the school on a team. The notes thanked us or congratulated us or encouraged us. They personally recognized us. Observers would hear her ringing your home if you were absent from class and visiting the hospital if your stupid leg had gone and broken itself while you were riding your new ten-speed.

If you were to make a checklist of her actions, it might be hard to recognize a pattern. Looking into your eyes—often. Smiling—often. Asking you why—often. Listening—often.

An observer would note that she never hugged or gushed. Hugging and gushing weren't her style. Neither did she yell nor scold nor belittle. Ever. But even the presence or absence of these behaviors does not describe Mrs. Farnell. Although she had the same general manner in teaching all of us, she made each of us feel as if she were teaching us in a very special way. She made each of us feel that.

In describing Mrs. Farnell, I want to turn from how she taught to how she treated us. No, to how she treated me.

That was it! As she looked at you with the brightest, bluest eyes this side of the Pacific and asked you if you'd had any trouble translating Plutarch, you knew she was caring about you.

And when, 15 years later, she found out you were divorced and broke and struggling to earn a doctorate in some sunny country that specialized in Disneyland and Harry Crews and Art Combs, she sent you a discreet loan, just enough to cover that impossible tuition fee and with it that note on paper that was the color and smell of lilacs. "Good luck, I'm so proud of you." You didn't feel quite so scared or alone.

And when, 31 years later, you anguished through the goodbye prayers at your own mother's funeral and were somehow drawn to look up and across the aisle into a pair of the brightest bluest eyes this side of the Pacific, you knew, again, how much Mrs. Farnell cared about you.

I've always wanted to scream my thank-you loud enough that she and everyone could hear, wherever in the world she was. Perhaps I just did.

References

Combs, A. (1965). *The Professional Education of Teachers.* Boston: Allyn and Bacon.

Combs, A. (1985). *A Personal Approach to Teaching: Beliefs That Make a Difference.* Boston: Allyn and Bacon.

Appendixes

OPTIONS:
Determining Type Preferences for Adolescents

Dr. Carolyn Marie Mamchur
Simon Fraser University

Directions

Prepare to answer some questions about yourself—the things you like and activities you enjoy.

There are no right or wrong answers to these questions. Try to give answers that show what **you** prefer.

For each sentence, choose the statement that you feel most comfortable with. Choose only **one** answer for each statement. If some choices are difficult, choose the one that would be correct most often.

Choose A or B for each statement.

I.

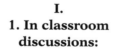

1. In classroom discussions:

A. I usually do the talking.

B. I talk only when needed.

2. When assigned a major project at school:

A. I work best on my own.

B. I like to check my ideas out with a group.

- **E**xtraversion
- **I**ntroversion
- **S**ensing
- i**N**tuition
- **T**hinking
- **F**eeling
- **J**udging
- **P**erceiving

**3. At the beginning
of the year:**

A. I wait until someone talks to me.

B. I start to talk to someone first.

**4. When my teachers are
asking questions in class:**

A. I usually like to answer right away and
know that I can get on the right track.

B. I like to think out my answer
and make sure it's right.

5. When I feel low:

A. I like to get away by myself to collect
my thoughts, like going for a drive
or watching TV.

B. I call up some of my friends
to go out and do something.

6. When it comes to friends, I have:

A. many, letting me do a variety of things with a variety of people.

B. one or two best friends, with whom I do most things.

7. I consider myself as:

A. daring.

B. cautious.

II.
1. I enjoy reading mostly:

A. fiction, novels, and plays.

B. non-fiction, such as biographies and how-to books.

- ■ **E**xtraversion
- ■ **I**ntroversion
- ■ **S**ensing
- ■ i**N**tuition
- ■ **T**hinking
- ■ **F**eeling
- ■ **J**udging
- ■ **P**erceiving

2. When writing a test, I would rather:

A. answer true or false, fill in the blanks, or select from multiple choices.

B. answer in sentences, paragraphs, or essays.

3. My friends come to me with their problems because:

A. they value my common sense.

B. they love to talk with me about possible solutions, no matter how unusual they might be.

4. I like to wear:

A. different clothing, trying new styles before anyone else, or inventing my own.

B. comfortable clothes that match.

5. An old cave is:

A. dirty and boring.

B. full of interesting things.

6. When listening to a story about something that happened while I was there:

A. I tend to get impatient with too many details. I want the person to get on with what the story is really about.

B. I tend to interrupt when the details aren't right.

7. I consider myself as:

A. good at noticing exactly what is happening right now.

B. good at guessing what might happen in a new situation

OPTIONS: Determining Type Preferences for Adolescents

119

- **E**xtraversion
- **I**ntroversion
- **S**ensing
- i**N**tuition
- **T**hinking
- **F**eeling
- **J**udging
- **P**erceiving

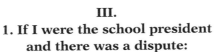

III.
1. If I were the school president and there was a dispute:

A. I would carefully examine what I believe to be right or wrong in this particular case, and try to do what is best for everyone.

B. I would refer to the school constitution (student rule book), analyzing what would be most fair.

2. Giving constructive criticism:

A. is a good way to help someone.

B. usually ends up in hurt feelings.

3. To have a good friendship:

A. it is better to tell the truth and keep things honest.

B. it might be better to hide the truth to spare someone's feelings and keep the peace.

**4. When a classroom rule has been
made and established:**

A. there is often a special circumstance that
makes it important to break that rule.

B. it is unfair to those who follow that rule
when the teacher lets someone break it.

**5. When determining a situation,
it is important to:**

A. see things as if they are
happening to me.

B. stand back and analyze it
as if I am an onlooker.

6. Time is well spent:

A. arguing over ideas and facts.

B. trying to understand and
support one another.

OPTIONS: Determining Type Preferences for Adolescents

■ **E**xtraversion
■ **I**ntroversion
■ **S**ensing
■ **iN**tuition
■ **T**hinking
■ **F**eeling
■ **J**udging
■ **P**erceiving

121

7. I am most upset by:

A. looking stupid.

B. being disliked.

IV.

**1. When it comes to keeping my things
(room, desk, clothes closet, papers):**

A. I have things organized; everything
has to be put in its proper place.

B. I have a system of my own that people
might say looks messy, but I know
exactly where everything is.

2. People might say to me:

A. "Lighten up."

B. "Shape up."

3. Teachers should:

A. Have everything planned.

B. Make sure students enjoy their work.

4. When given a range of assignments:

A. I like to explore several topics
until I get excited about one.

B. I need to make a definite choice
and get to work as fast as I can.

5. When on a camping trip:

A. I like to rough out a few things I'd like to
do, knowing that I can always change my
mind at the last minute.

B. I like to have a good plan
and stick to it.

■ **E**xtraversion

■ **I**ntroversion

■ **S**ensing

■ i**N**tuition

■ **T**hinking

■ **F**eeling

■ **J**udging

■ **P**erceiving

6. Teachers should:

A. Set down the rules.

B. Talk things over with students.

7. I prefer being:

A. decisive.

B. curious.

Scoring Your Choices

For each section, select the type code (E or I, S or N, T or F, J or P) that defines your learning preference.

SECTION I

Turn back to your answer sheet and circle the same answers on this sheet.

1.	A = [E]	B = [I]
2.	A = [I]	B = [E]
3.	A = [I]	B = [E]
4.	A = [E]	B = [I]
5.	A = [I]	B = [E]
6.	A = [E]	B = [I]
7.	A = [E]	B = [I]

Add up the number of E's and the number of I's.

Number of E's _____   Number of I's _____

If you have chosen four (4) or more E's, give yourself an "E" next to "**SECTION I**" below.
If you have chosen four (4) or more I's, give yourself an "I" next to "**SECTION I**" below.

SECTION I _____

SECTION II

Turn back to your answer sheet and circle the same answers on this sheet.

1.	A = [N]	B = [S]
2.	A = [S]	B = [N]
3.	A = [S]	B = [N]
4.	A = [N]	B = [S]
5.	A = [S]	B = [N]
6.	A = [N]	B = [S]
7.	A = [S]	B = [N]

Add up the number of S's and the number of N's.

Number of S's _____   Number of N's _____

If you have chosen four (4) or more S's, give yourself an "S" next to "**SECTION II**" below.
If you have chosen four (4) or more N's, give yourself an "N" next to "**SECTION II**" below.

SECTION II _____

OPTIONS: Determining Type Preferences for Adolescents

125

■ **E**xtraversion
■ **I**ntroversion
■ **S**ensing
■ i**N**tuition
■ **T**hinking
■ **F**eeling
■ **J**udging
■ **P**erceiving

SECTION III

Turn back to your answer sheet and circle the same answers on this sheet.

1.   A = [F]   B = [T]
2.   A = [T]   B = [F]
3.   A = [T]   B = [F]
4.   A = [F]   B = [T]
5.   A = [F]   B = [T]
6.   A = [T]   B = [F]
7.   A = [T]   B = [F]

Add up the number of T's and the number of F's.

Number of T's _____   Number of F's _____

If you have chosen four (4) or more T's, give yourself a "T" next to "**SECTION III**" below.
If you have chosen four (4) or more F's, give yourself an "F" next to "**SECTION III**" below.

SECTION III _____

SECTION IV

Turn back to your answer sheet and circle the same answers on this sheet.

1.   A = [J]   B = [P]
2.   A = [J]   B = [P]
3.   A = [J]   B = [P]
4.   A = [P]   B = [J]
5.   A = [P]   B = [J]
6.   A = [J]   B = [P]
7.   A = [J]   B = [P]

Add up the number of J's and the number of P's.

Number of J's _____   Number of P's _____

If you have chosen four (4) or more J's, give yourself a "J" next to "**SECTION IV**" below.
If you have chosen four (4) or more P's, give yourself a "P" next to "**SECTION IV**" below.

SECTION IV _____

YOU HAVE CHOSEN THE TYPE ___ ___ ___ ___. (Write down the letters you chose for each section, I, II, III, and IV. This will give you four initials.) Turn to the next page to discover which "type" you feel you are at this stage in your life.

Brief Descriptions of the Sixteen Types as They Apply to Students

ENTJ

Ambitious, aggressive, critical. Easily bored with routine repetition, they thrive on intellectual conflict, but deeply resent ever being made to look incompetent. They enjoy a challenge, are highly competitive, and love to win. Gregarious and outgoing, they are natural leaders despite their tendency to be openly critical and capable of mockery. Well organized and tenacious, they usually get the job done, whatever that job is.

ISFP

Observant, considerate, patient. They shun disagreement, value harmony, learn best with hands-on learning from a teacher they like in a setting that is caring and safe. Loyal and helpful, they enjoy subjects that are pragmatic and useful in the larger sense. Easily overlooked, they need encouragement to perform. They are the last to appreciate their own virtues and abilities. Sensitive to nuance, keenly aware of everything that goes on around them, they are great barometers of mood in a classroom setting.

ESTJ

Practical, hard working, determined. Needing schedules and wanting to plan ahead, they appreciate a well-organized teacher who is consistent and fair. They enjoy hands-on activities, may have trouble with theoretical concepts, appreciate specific examples when working on any topic. Naturally bossy, they enjoy being in charge. They enjoy, too, a teacher who is clearly in control of the classroom.

INFP

Imaginative, idealistic, reflective. Highly independent, they appreciate a flexible school program that offers plenty of opportunity for following their own creative inclinations. Loyal to ideals, they can be very stubborn if forced to do something they don't believe in or have no interest in doing. They enjoy working with and for others, but on their own terms. Easily hurt, they are very sensitive to criticism of any kind.

■ **E**xtraversion
■ **I**ntroversion
■ **S**ensing
■ **iN**tuition
■ **T**hinking
■ **F**eeling
■ **J**udging
■ **P**erceiving

INTP

Curious, analytical, independent. They are relentless in learning about things they care about, indifferent to things they don't. They enjoy going deeply into subjects, exploring their own ideas. Often labeled as gifted or as underachievers, they work to their own rules. Highly analytical and critical, they only respect and cooperate with teachers who consistently show intelligence, expertise, and fairness. Natural scientists, they are the most inventive of all the types.

ESFJ

Sociable, opinionated, orderly. They learn best in a friendly, interactive structure in which they know what is expected and can please the teacher. Willing participants in classroom activities, they place a high value on having things completed and on receiving feedback from the teacher. They enjoy learning activities in which they can be actively engaged with others. Well organized and responsible, they are very good students.

ISTP

Cool, curious observers of life. They hate waste of anything: time, energy, talk. They learn best by observing firsthand in a one-on-one real-world situation. Independent, focused, realistic, they shun what they see as fake, creative, artsy projects. They often learn without a teacher or school, applying themselves diligently to those practical things they care about. Natural troubleshooters, lovers of adventure, they may cause upsets just to relieve the boredom.

ENFJ

Expressive, opinionated, caring, conscientious. Wanting to excel and wanting to please the teacher, they are model students, especially for teachers they like. Deeply hurt by criticism, they crave praise for themselves and others. Imaginative and intense, they enjoy learning and achievement. They often take on leadership positions in the school, thereby satisfying their dual urge to be in charge and to take care of others.

ESTP Easygoing, curious, adaptive. They enjoy hands-on, realistic, practical learning situations in which the subject matter relates directly to their own interests. Full of restless energy, impatient with theory, they appreciate teachers who are themselves energetic and flexible and who can make learning fun. They can be disruptive unless the teacher can challenge their imaginative energy and good-natured love of pleasure.	**INFJ** Serious, quietly forceful, and persevering. They have a strong love of learning and do well academically. They enjoy reading and writing and communicate clearly and with passion. Natural crusaders, they bring enthusiastic leadership and diligence to any cause they believe in. Enjoying personal attention, they become model students, combining independent reflection and active, respectful participation.
ESFP Friendly, easygoing, fun-loving, and enthusiastic. They want to enjoy all life, including school life. They like to learn by actively participating in group projects. They want to create personal relationships with everyone, including teachers. Upset by conflict, they need a friendly, sociable learning environment where they feel the teacher has a genuine interest in them and in practical, nontheoretical subjects.	**INTJ** Critical, serious, decisive to the point of stubbornness. They learn best when given freedom to learn what and how they want. Loving challenge, resenting rote memory, they naturally gravitate toward sources of higher learning— libraries, experts, concert halls. Intensely introspective, they set their own standards of excellence and can be very self-critical and demanding. They enjoy the idea of a thing as much as actually doing it and can spend too much time in internal reverie.

- **E**xtraversion
- **I**ntroversion
- **S**ensing
- i**N**tuition
- **T**hinking
- **F**eeling
- **J**udging
- **P**erceiving

ISTJ

Decisive, dependable, systematic. Thorough and painstaking, they apply themselves to subjects they consider useful. Precise and accurate, they value precision and accuracy, resenting error and vagueness. Skeptical, they mistrust easy affection, easy learning, easy success. Quick to criticize, they can be hard on teachers, on friends, on themselves. They apply themselves dutifully when they see a practical value to the learning.

ENFP

Warmly enthusiastic, creative, and charismatic. They bring a great energy to all aspects of their lives, including the classroom. They love to discover and will put tremendous energy into projects where they have the freedom to do research, explore in depth, produce new ideas. Wanting to please, to be a part of things, they join activities with intensity and passion. Easily carried away, they may need help in limiting themselves and sticking to deadlines.

ISFJ

Caring, dedicated, dependable, stable, and conservative. They put tremendous and painstaking energy into projects that affect others. Concerned about the welfare of their peers, their school, their teacher, their world, they focus energy with great passion. Expert at collecting sensory data, they love to observe and imitate. They want the classroom to be well organized and considerate. They believe there are rules to classroom life and expect the teacher to enforce them.

ENTP

Highly individual, innovative, and enthusiastic. They accept any challenge with vigor and a firm belief in their ability to succeed. Impulsive and energetic, relentless in their passion to understand and inspire, they can be almost ruthless in their quest to give and receive knowledge. Competitive and critical, they themselves cannot bear to look incompetent and deeply resent anyone who puts them in that position.

Glossary

E	Extraversion:	an external focus of interest and energy.
I	Introversion:	an internal focus of interest and energy.
S	Sensing:	a direct, practical, focused attention to detail using the five senses.
N	Intuition:	an indirect, future-oriented attention to broad issues through seeking patterns and relationships.
T	Thinking:	an objective, analytical approach to problem solving.
F	Feeling:	a subjective, values-oriented approach to problem solving.
J	Judging:	an organized, closure-driven way to deal with the world.
P	Perceiving	a flexible, curiosity-driven way to deal with the world.

SJ   The Traditionalist, driven by a need to serve, to do one's duty well, to guard the system.

NT   The Promethean Achiever, driven by the need to be perfect, to seek ultimate knowledge and competency.

NF   The Idealistic Change Agent, driven by a need for integrity and exploration.

SP   The Dionysian Free Spirit, driven by a need to be free to do whatever is immediately of value.

These initials, when combined, form the 16 types:

■ **E**xtraversion
■ **I**ntroversion
■ **S**ensing
■ i**N**tuition
■ **T**hinking
■ **F**eeling
■ **J**udging
■ **P**erceiving

ISTJ	INFJ
ISFJ	INTJ
ISTP	INFP
ISFP	INTP
ESTP	ENFP
ESFP	ENTP
ESTJ	ENFJ
ESFJ	ENTJ

In addition to the 8 type code initials and the resulting 16 types, several acronyms appear in this book:

AORO: Action Oriented, Reflection Oriented. An observation instrument to determine extraversion or introversion in students.

CAPT: Center for Applications of Psychological Type. A research center in Gainesville, Florida.

I.I.I.: Instant Insight Inventory. A short form self-scoring questionnaire to determine Jungian preference in adults.

MBTI: Myers-Briggs Type Indicator. A 166-item forced-answer questionnaire used to determine type preferences.

OPTIONS: A self-scoring questionnaire that students use to determine their learning style preferences.

PROFILE: Extensive descriptions of an individual in the workplace, based on MBTI scores.

About the Author

Born in Saskatchewan in the 1940s, Carolyn Mamchur was a mother, wife, high school teacher and university student by her twentieth birthday. She left Canada for Florida to earn a doctorate in education in 1976 and begin her writing career working with the Southern author Harry Crews. Now an associate professor at Simon Fraser University and president of her own company, Carolyn completed her postdoctorate work at the Jung Institute in Switzerland and gives extensive lectures and workshops on writing process, Jungian type theory, implementation processes, motivational needs and stress management, and organizational development. She is the author of several books and seven screenplays, and has just completed a children's book, *The Popcorn Tree*, which is being released by Stoddard. She lives with her daughter and two dogs in Vancouver and all four escape to their cabin in Washington as often as possible.

Profiles, other materials, and workshops on type theory are available from C. Mamchur & Associates, 3488 W. 3rd Ave., Vancouver, B.C., V6K 1L5. Phone: 604-734-4072. Fax: 604-736-4060.